T0127721

# *More* MEDITATIONS *from* A PASTOR'S HEART

Spirit-Filled Sermon Outlines for Pastors,
Preachers, and Teachers of the Word of God

BOOK 2

Jerome A. Jochem M.S., M.A.

WESTBOW
PRESS®
A DIVISION OF THOMAS NELSON
& ZONDERVAN

Scripture taken from the King James Version of the Bible.

Scripture taken from the New Century Version®. Copyright © 2005 by Thomas Nelson. Used by permission. All rights reserved.

Scripture quotations marked (NIV) are taken from the Holy Bible, New International Version®, NIV®. Copyright © 1973, 1978, 1984, 2011 by Biblica, Inc.™ Used by permission of Zondervan. All rights reserved worldwide. www.zondervan.com The "NIV" and "New International Version" are trademarks registered in the United States Patent and Trademark Office by Biblica, Inc.™

WestBow Press books may be ordered through booksellers or by contacting:

WestBow Press
A Division of Thomas Nelson & Zondervan
1663 Liberty Drive
Bloomington, IN 47403
www.westbowpress.com
1 (866) 928-1240

ISBN: 978-1-9736-3375-4 (sc)
ISBN: 978-1-9736-3374-7 (e)

Print information available on the last page.

WestBow Press rev. date: 08/06/2018

# Dedication

I dedicate this work to my beloved wife, Roxie and to my children, Molly, Crystal, and Faith. I specifically dedicate this book to my grandchildren, Andrew, Dylan, Heather, Alex, Jean, Isaac, William, Sommer, Chaney, Dixie, and Zach.

# Preface

The Bible is truly an amazing book. It has so many levels of meaning that its content seems endless. I have been preaching for 27 years, at the time that I wrote this book. I have truly preached a lot of sermons over a wide range of circumstances. I have found it unnecessary to preach the same sermon twice since the Bible provides new understanding and insight through the Holy Spirit each time I sit down to write a sermon.

This is book 2 of my sermon outline series, and as in book 1, I would like to share just a very few of the sermons that the Holy Spirit has given me for my church. These outlines will be of great value to pastors, preachers, teachers, small group leaders, and to anyone who would use them for personal devotions or meditations. I am sure that you will find the insights and truths outlined in this book to be useful in reaching both the churched and unchurched in your community. Remember that these are sermon outlines and you will need to fill them in with the message that God is giving you for your church, bible study group, or home group.

I am a pastor who has been baptized in the Holy Spirit and so some of my sermon outlines point to the empowering and gifting that comes with this experience. If you belong to a denomination which does not teach the Baptism of the Holy Spirit as an experience independent of salvation, you will still find many of these outlines to be useful as you preach about the basics concerning our Lord Jesus Christ.

Finally, I pray that you will be inspired and made joyful by these sermon outlines. Several times during my 27 years of preaching and teaching, I entered a dry spell and needed inspiration and encouragement. Preachers, pastors, and teachers all get writer's block, and it is my prayer that these sermon outlines will help you through such difficult times. May the Lord bless you with new insight, aspirations, and greater faith in Jesus as you use these sermon outlines to minister to God's people.

Pastor **Jerome A. Jochem M.S., M.A.**

# Contents

# *One*

# FOUR KEYS TO UNDERSTANDING THE LIGHT OF GOD

**T**ext: *⁷But if we live in the light, as God is in the light, we can share fellowship with each other. Then the blood of Jesus, God's Son, cleanses us from every sin.* **1 John 1:7 (NCV)**

## INTRODUCTION:
There are several fundamental concepts found in this Scripture, and I would like to discuss each with you so that we can better understand the light of God.

## THE LIGHT IS LOVE:
*²Live a life of love just as Christ loved us and gave himself for us as a sweet-smelling offering and sacrifice to God.* **Ephesians 5:2 (NCV)**
- A Greek word for love is "Agape." The underlying nature of agape is the unconditional giving of oneself for the sake of others, both Christian and non-Christian. It is an unselfish and selfless action that benefits others.
- If you are in the light, then your life is filled with love. This love is the passion of a servant whose primary desire is to serve others. Our example for this is Christ who loved us to the point of death, but who was also a servant to his twelve apostles.
- Another Greek word for love is "Philo," which in Greek means brotherly or affectionate love. When Jesus reinstated Simon Peter after his resurrection, Jesus asked Peter if Peter loved him (Agape love). Peter responded by saying that he had an affectionate or brotherly love for Jesus (Philo love). Jesus requested that Peter

agape his sheep and Peter wished to reassure Jesus that he had brotherly love for Jesus, a love that was also shared by Jesus for Peter. (John 21:16 – 17).

- A key to understanding living a life of love is that the more we philo Christ, the more we can agape others.

## THE LIGHT IS TRUTH:

*⁶As you received Christ Jesus the Lord, so continue to live in him.⁷Keep your roots deep in him and have your lives built on him. Be strong in the faith, just as you were taught, and always be thankful. ⁸Be sure that no one leads you away with false and empty teaching that is only human, which comes from the ruling spirits of this world, and not from Christ.⁹All of God lives in Christ fully (even when Christ was on earth),¹⁰and you have a full and true life in Christ, who is ruler over all rulers and powers.* **Colossians 2:6-10 (NCV)**

- When we receive Jesus Christ as Lord, that means that we make his will our priority and goal in life.
- The way that Christ sees our world is the truth. God's perception or way of seeing the world is radically different from that of humanity. No matter how complicated our lives become, the truth of Christ must rule.
- For truth to dominate, we must know what we believe, based on the Word of God and not on a compromise of what the Word says.
- If we allow the world to compromise the Word, then we will suffer from false theologies and teachings. Compromise truth, and it will not be difficult to lose the gospel and the central message of salvation and holy living.
- This Scripture points to the fact that we must follow divine wisdom instead of worldly wisdom because Christ's truth is absolute.

## THE LIGHT IS SPIRIT:

*¹⁶So I tell you: Live by following the Spirit. Then you will not do what your sinful selves want. ¹⁷Our sinful selves want what is against the Spirit, and the Spirit wants what is against our sinful selves. The two are against each* *other, so you cannot do just what you please. $^{18}$But if the Spirit is leading you, you are not under the law.* **Galatians 5:16-18 (NCV)**

While our salvation is dependent on faith in the work of Jesus Christ, the bridge between our consciousness of God and God is the person of the Holy Spirit.

- It is critical for every Christian to have a direct line to Christ and his father through the presence of the Holy Spirit.
- Jesus told us that the Holy Spirit would be our guide and our teacher, so it is imperative that we establish contact with the Holy Spirit through the Baptism of the Holy Spirit. (John 16:7 – 13).
- When we live by following the Holy Spirit, we reject the demands of sin in our lives. It is through the power of the Holy Spirit that we can live comparatively sin-free lives.
- Usually, when we fall into sin, it is because we have not drawn upon the Holy Spirit to overcome the temptation to sin.
- By doing what the Holy Spirit wants instead of doing what we want, we can live the Christian life as modeled by Jesus Christ. Without the help of the Holy Spirit, such a lifestyle would be impossible for our weak flesh under the law of judgment.

## THE LIGHT IS WISDOM AND UNDERSTANDING:

$^{9}$*Because of this, since the day we heard about you, we have continued praying for you, asking God that you will know fully what he wants. We pray that you will also have great wisdom and understanding in spiritual things $^{10}$so that you will live the kind of life that honors and pleases the Lord in every way.* **Colossians 1:9-10 (NCV)**

The universe is very complicated, and we live complicated lives in that fantastic and mind-numbing reality we call our world.

- We need wisdom not only to live productively but also to understand and comprehend the dynamics of the spiritual universe. In other words, we need to know how to live correctly here, and by doing so, please God at the same time.
- No matter how many mistakes we make, if God knows that in our hearts we want to please him, he will help us overcome our mistakes and live a holy life. A prime example of that is David,

3

who committed adultery and murder, but once he confessed his sins, God helped him to remain "a man after God's heart."

- There is hope for us that we can please and honor the one who died for us because he loved us.

## CONCLUSION:

If we understand the four concepts of love, we can live in a way that pleases God, blesses our brothers and sisters in Christ, and maintains a daily relationship with Jesus Christ based on our love for him and his children. It begins with love, flows into a relationship, increases wisdom, and ends in honor. This is a perfect description of the lifestyle of a Christian who desires to please God.

## NOTES:

# THE EMOTIONS OF JESUS

**T**ext: *⁴¹As he approached Jerusalem and saw the city, he wept over it.* **John 19:41 (NIV)**

## INTRODUCTION:

I think most Christians identify Christ as the Son of God, remote and emotionally distant from the common feelings that you and I have. While it is true, that Jesus was the only begotten Son of God and God in himself, he also was a fully human being with a full set of emotions that he expressed during the time of his ministry.

Of the four Gospels, the Gospel of Mark tends to give not only a description of Jesus's actions but also his feelings. We also must look in the other Gospels for clues to see how emotionally sensitive Jesus was to his situation. Recognizing his emotions helps us to identify with our Lord when we realize that he experienced the same kind of emotions that we experience and can relate to our feelings. In this sermon, I'm going to preach about several emotions that Jesus showed us during his lifetime so that we can relate to them and him with a greater understanding and appreciation of his humanity.

## THE LOVING JESUS:

*²³Jesus answered, "If people love me, they will obey my teaching. My Father will love them, and we will come to them and make our home with them.* **John 14:23 (NCV)**

Jerome A. Jochem M.S., M.A.

The Bible tells us that God's love is without limit. His love for us exists today and will exist throughout all eternity.

- Although God's love is unlimited, experiencing it is not unconditional - you must accept it!
- Jesus's purpose was to illustrate God's love for us with great determination. A determination that carried him to the cross to fulfill the requirements of his Father.
- To fully accept and experience the love of Christ, we must first love God, and secondly, love each other.
- The passport to both heaven and God's kingdom is the love of Christ.

## THE ANGRY JESUS:
*Jesus was angry as he looked at the people, and he felt very sad because they were stubborn. Then he said to the man, "Hold out your hand. "The man held out his hand, and it was healed.* **Mark 3:5 (NCV).**

Many people expect God to be angry. In fact, I believe that more people expect an angry God rather than a loving God.

- In this situation, Jesus is angry at the hardheartedness of the people who were accusing him of breaking the law by healing on a Sabbath, or at least not defending him for healing on the Sabbath.
- A passion for people to have the right values and understanding of God's love motivated his anger.
- He was angry because the people thought that keeping the Sabbath is more important than relieving human suffering.

## THE GRIEVING JESUS:
[33]*When Jesus saw Mary crying and the Jews who came with her also weeping, he was upset and was deeply troubled.* [34]*He asked, "Where did you bury him?" "Come and see, Lord," they said.* [35]*Jesus cried.* **John 11:33-35 (NCV)**

Jesus was about 33 years of age when he was ministering in Israel, and by that time he had witnessed the death of his adoptive father, Joseph, and probably other people and relatives.

- Although he had grieved before when Joseph died, he was not able to do anything about death because it was not his time to reveal himself.
- When Lazarus died, he experienced the full force of grief, and like any other person who loved Lazarus, he began to suffer from personal loss and compassion for those people who also loved Lazarus.
- From this story, we understand that grief did not paralyze Jesus, but love brought Lazarus back to life.

## THE INDIGNANT JESUS:

*[14]When Jesus saw this, he was upset and said to them, "Let the little children come to me. Don't stop them, because the kingdom of God belongs to people who are like these children.* **Mark 10:14 (NCV)**

By keeping the children away from Jesus, the apostles violated the wish of Christ to minister to them, and this brought about a feeling of anger. The apostles took authority which they did not have, and they misused that authority by preventing the children from being ministered to by Christ.

- I believe that Jesus still becomes indignant when someone prevents either a child or an adult from committing to him and therefore losing their opportunity to be saved.
- Although Christ was not obligated to share his reasoning, note that he stated that even children have a right to access salvation.
- The haughty authority assumed by the apostles may have disqualified them from heaven, while the children's humility qualified them to be citizens of heaven.

## THE FRUSTRATED JESUS:

*[12]Jesus sighed deeply and said, "Why do you people ask for a miracle as a sign? I tell you the truth; no sign will be given to you."* **Mark 8:12 (NCV)**

In this Scripture, Jesus is showing that he is deeply frustrated with the people who would not believe unless they had a "sign." One becomes frustrated when one's desires or one's goals are blocked by other people or by bad attitudes.

- During this time in his ministry, Jesus was preaching his heart out, giving the people the message of God's love, passionately loving them, healing them, feeding them, forgiving them, and yet they asked for a "sign."

- Asking him for a "sign" meant that they did not believe him, and so he told them the only sign that they would <u>have</u> is his resurrection.

## THE SORROWFUL JESUS:

³ *He was hated and rejected by people. He had much pain and suffering. People would not even look at him. He was hated, and we didn't even notice him.* **Isaiah 53:3 (NCV)**

This Scripture is from the Old Testament, and it is prophetic concerning the emotions experienced by the Messiah because of the rejection of the people of Israel.

- He would experience rejection, emotional as well as physical pain and suffering. He suffered the punishment of being a social outcast, and the anxiety of being hated and was eventually murdered because of it.
- All these emotions produced great sorrow in Jesus. Sadness for the people of Israel who would reject their Savior, and in Jerusalem, the spiritual capital of Israel, for the rejection of the Messiah and king.

## THE JOYFUL JESUS:

²¹ *Then Jesus rejoiced in the Holy Spirit and said, "I praise you, Father, Lord of heaven and earth because you have hidden these things from the people who are wise and smart. But you have shown them to those who are like little children. Yes, Father, this is what you really wanted.* **Luke 10:21 (NCV)**

The proper definition of the word rejoiced in this Scripture means "to jump with joy." In other words, he danced with joy.

- In this Scripture, we see Jesus genuinely moved by a passionate spirit felt joy because his disciples had gotten the message and had walked in faith in his power.
- Note that the basis of this joy was his father's action to reveal spiritual truth to those who are humble as children. Jesus was joyful to the point of dance because his father's will was done.

## THE COMPASSIONATE JESUS:

[36] *When he saw the crowds, he felt sorry for them because they were hurting and helpless, like sheep without a shepherd.* **Matthew 9:36 (NCV)**

Compassion is more than just an intellectual sympathy. Empathy is an emotion which acts as a motivator for action. Jesus had compassion because the people of Israel had great burdens under Rome and their "establishment" religious organization.

- He came to be the shepherd of the many sheep who did not have a true shepherd. A true shepherd is the one who offers his life for the benefit of his sheep.
- Even today, the primary characteristic of a good under-shepherd of Christ is compassion.

## THE GENTLE JESUS:

[29] *Accept my teachings and learn from me, because I am gentle and humble in spirit, and you will find rest for your lives.* **Matthew 11:29 (NCV)**

Being gentle and humble are not only behaviors, but they are also attitudes, and emotions.
What Jesus is saying here is that the people of Israel who were also humble and meek should identify with Jesus and accept his teachings.

- Although Christ, as we have seen, expressed a wide variety of emotions including passionate anger, he never was aggressive towards people in expressing those feelings.
- The practice of the behavior, the attitude, and the emotions concerning humility and gentleness is a protector against violence both physical and verbal

## CONCLUSION:

In this sermon, I intended to show that Jesus experienced a wide variety of emotions. Because he was a full human being, he has personal and intimate knowledge of our feelings. Even though we may not receive a lot of understanding from other people, we can depend on Christ to understand how we feel. Not only does Christ understand our feelings, but he will share his feelings with us, and often those feelings become our guidelines to live a life which pleases God. Christianity is not, nor can it ever be just an intellectual religion. Christianity is filled with the power of emotion.

**Notes:**

# Three

# OUR CARING GOD

**T**ext: *⁷Cast all your anxiety on him because he cares for you.* **1 Peter 5:8 (NIV)**

## INTRODUCTION:

There are many Scriptures, both in the Old and New Testament that state we are to trust the Lord when we are afraid or anxious, and we are to place those anxieties upon him. (Proverbs 3:5 – 6, Philippians 4:6 – 7). Our Scripture for today from 1 Peter tells us why we should cast our anxieties and fears upon the Lord. It proclaims that we should do these things because he cares for us. In this sermon, I would like to discuss what it means to have a God who cares.

## TO CARE:

The word "care" in the Greek language means "to be concerned" or "to be of interest to." We should cast our cares and anxieties upon God because he is concerned about us and interested in our lives. This is a remarkable idea for many reasons:

- Regarding our position in the cosmos, we are utterly insignificant, and yet God is concerned about us.
- Regarding our position compared to all of humanity, God is interested in our individual lives.

It is a mind-blowing fact that the Almighty God of the cosmos, the one who made our vast universe, who is all-knowing, all-powerful, and ever-present takes an interest in our lives.

Jerome A. Jochem M.S., M.A.

## THE IMPACT OF CARING:

God expresses the fact that he cares for us in different ways.

- He will forgive us our sins when we confess and repent.
- He will show us mercy and compassion.
- He will intercede in our lives to change them for the better, according to his plans for us.
- He will always care which means that he will never abandon or leave us.
- He will love us to the end.

## THE ROLE OF TRUST:

The fact that God cares for us has a direct impact on our trust or in our faith in him.

- If we don't believe that God cares for us and is willing to act on our behalf, then we will never trust him with our lives or with our problems. Instead, we will try to solve our problems by ourselves. We fail in most cases because we do not have the power to implement the solution.
- If we do not believe that God cares for us, then we are not motivated to care for him. To care for a person implies a relationship, and if a person feels that he is not loved, any connection will be weak at best.
- Without a fundamental understanding that God cares for us as individuals, our concept of God may be that of a remote, distant, and punishing deity. Such a god will not be trusted, but will instead cause fear in the most negative sense of the word.

## CONCLUSION:

It is fair to say that God's position towards us is one of loving concern. Because he cares for us, we always have him on our side, and he is willing to intervene for us to help us overcome those fears, anxieties, and problems that we face as we live our daily lives. Our prayer should be that we learn to appreciate and depend on his loving concern because he genuinely does care for us.

NOTES:

# Four

# UNION WITH CHRIST

**T**ext: *⁵⁶Those who eat my flesh and drink my blood live in me, and I live in them.* **John 6:56 (NCV)**

## INTRODUCTION:

Many times one of the most potent aspects of salvation is ignored. Our union with Christ is essential to our Christian faith, but it is often misunderstood or just set aside as a worthy topic. In this sermon, I would like to discuss just a few crucial concepts about our union with Christ.

## IS OUR UNION WITH CHRIST REAL?

To answer this question, we must examine the many Scriptures which support the idea of union with Christ. The Scriptures use two types of phrases to indicate our union with Christ.

1.  The phrase "We are in Christ." may be found in 2 Corinthians 5:17, John 15:4, 5, 7; 1 Corinthians 15:22; 3 Corinthians 12:1; Galatians 3:28; Ephesians 1:4, 2:10; Philippians 3:9; 1 Thessalonians 4:16; and 1 John 4:13.
2.  The phrase "Christ is in us." may be found in Galatians 2:20; Colossians 1:27; Romans 8:10; 2 Corinthians 13:5; and Ephesians 3:17.

In addition to these references, several Scriptures were written by John that combined both phrases and their underlying ideas. (John 6:56; John 15:4; 1 John 4:13) So, just based on the number of references, primarily from Paul, we can comfortably conclude that while it is difficult to understand the concept of union with Christ, that union is valid and actual.

## WHAT IS OUR UNION WITH CHRIST?

Union with Christ is part of the salvation experience. Before salvation, there is a barrier between God and the lost person. That barrier is the sin in the life of the person. Sin breaks fellowship with God.

God still loves the lost person, but while the person is unforgiven, there is no chance of a relationship with him.

The Lord Jesus came to remove that barrier, and when a person commits to him, a relationship is instantly established. Christ is in the person, and the person is in Christ, and that is the union promised in the Scriptures. Our union with Christ has two dimensions:

1. The physical aspect in which each believer becomes a member of the body of Christ. They become part of his church, and by doing so become his hands, mouth, and feet.
2. The spiritual aspect in which Christ and the believer are made as one by their mutual love for each other.

## WHAT ARE THE BENEFITS OF UNION WITH CHRIST?

When we talk about the benefits of our union with Christ, we are talking about the benefits of salvation.

- To describe those benefits, we use such theological terms as forgiveness, justification, righteousness, adoption, and sanctification.
- Essentially, none of the benefits of being saved could apply to us if there is no union with Christ. When we have union with Christ, the benefits are ours because he is the source of them and each comes from him.

The new creation, the new life, and the revitalized person that we become after salvation are all due to our union with Christ. We are in him, and he is in us, and that means we can rejoice in our new identity.

## IS UNION A FEELING OR AN EXPERIENCE?

Once we experience salvation, we can experience Jesus on a personal level. Our union with him is expressed by:

- A sense of divine presence and companionship.
- A new understanding of the Word as it is illuminated to us intellectually.

- A new and more vigorous prayer life because now we have him in us and it is easier to talk to him.
- A growing ability to love as we experience his love for us.
- A more dynamic and pressing need to serve him through his church.

So, our union with Christ is not only a theological concept but has a real and powerful effect on our emotions and thoughts. Our union is both experiential and emotional.

## How do I Intensify our Union?

A similar question is how do you intensify your relationship with anyone you love and who loves you?

- Talk to the Christ in you. Talking is just praying with the knowledge that he hears you since he is in union with you.
- Serve the Christ in you. Service is an essential way of strengthening your union with Christ because you need to listen to him, submit to his will, and obey him.
- Read the Word about your union with him. The Word of God will give you all the information and guidance that you need. Be sure to allow the Holy Spirit to illuminate the Word instead of using the interpretations of men.
- Allow the love of Christ in you to flow to others. The love of Christ is all you have and all you need to love others. Even if you do not like a person, you can love them with the love of Christ in you.

## Conclusion:

The fact of the matter is that Christ is in you and you are in him. The union that you have with him is the most powerful aspect of your Christianity. As such, your union needs to be strengthened, rejoiced in, and lived each day. Your Lord and Savior lives in you and is yours for all eternity because you are also in him.

## Notes:

# The Anguish of a Father
# - The Cry of a Prophet

**Text:** *³³Then the king was very upset, and he went to the room over the city gate and cried. As he went, he cried out, "My son Absalom, my son Absalom! I wish I had died and not you. Absalom, my son, my son!"* **2 Samuel 18:33 (NCV)**

## Introduction:

The Old Testament contains the history of many families, and through these family histories, we see how fathers have treated their sons and daughters. The New Testament tends to focus on God our Father through his relationship with his son, our Lord, and Savior, Jesus Christ. So, the Old Testament is rich with insight as to how human fathers should treat their children, and one of the most moving and insightful stories in the Old Testament is that of David's relationship with his son Absalom.

## About Absalom:

Absalom was the third son of David. According to Scripture, he was an incredibly handsome young man (2 Samuel 14:25), and his mother was royalty. Both qualities may have contributed to his character defects.

## What defects of character?

Nowadays Absalom would be considered a problem child. He indeed was self-centered and self-willed without any compassion or mercy for those around him.

1. He was a murderer in that he arranged for the death of his brother Amnon because he hated Amnon for raping his sister

Tamar. Now, Absalom did not "plunge the knife," but he did tell others to attack and kill Amnon. (2 Samuel 13:22 – 29) After he murdered Amnon, he ran away to his mother's kingdom entirely deserting Israel, rather than face the consequences of his actions. (2 Samuel 13:37 – 38)

2. Eventually, David permitted Absalom to return to Israel. But when he returned, he began to betray his father, David, by conspiring to steal the kingdom of Israel from David's control. He did this by winning the hearts of the men of Israel. (2 Samuel 15: 13) So, Absalom is not only a murderer; he was a betrayer committing the highest form of treason against his father.

## DAVID'S LOVE:

The most amazing characteristics of David's love is that despite Absalom's terrible behavior, David continues to love him through each incident. David forgave him, tried to reconcile with him, and finally commanded his army to show mercy to Absalom, even though Absalom had rebelled against his position as King of Israel.

Like David's love, a characteristic of a father's love is that it is unconditional. Love does not depend on the performance of the child but is continuously given to the child, even during the time of appalling and disobedient behavior.

- A father is responsible for disciplining his child but withdrawing his love can do the child more damage than good.
- Fathers, if you have a child who is a great disappointment to you, then you must be patient and consistently love them with a love that only a father can give.
- Remember that you are the only one who can love as a real father and that through your love your child will learn to love his children.

Despite the evil Absalom did, David's love for Absalom illustrates God the Father's love for us despite the harm that we have done. The Father God's love for us is unconditional, and that means that even when we disappoint ourselves, and we disappoint him by sin, he is willing to forgive us and reconcile with us. All we need to do is confess, repent, and have faith in his love for us through Christ.

## FROM DAD TO GOD:

We often get our image of God our Heavenly Father based on our relationship with our human fathers. Good relations produce a good picture of God the Father, but it is also true that a weak relationship spells difficulty in establishing our relationship with God the Father.

- Human fathers often distance themselves from their children because of their focus on success. That success has very little to do with how good a father we are to our children.
- David was a victorious king. David was a successful musician. David was a successful poet. David was a successful administrator, but he was not a successful father.
- When fathers entirely focus on making a living or being a success in a career, they tend to become emotionally distant from their children. They don't provide the fatherly love that sons and daughters need, and as a result, these children cannot identify with God's love because God is just another remote and distant father figure.

The only solution to this problem is to spend as much time with your children as you spend being a success. Fathers need to show their kids, but especially their sons, love. He must take the time to reassure his kids that he loves them, and give them the support they need to grow up to be healthy adults. With David, it was too late to change the heart of Absalom, for many of us fathers, we need to act now and not wait for another day to pass.

## THE FATHER'S RESPONSIBILITY:

The Bible tells us that we are responsible for training up our children, so they have the moral and spiritual knowledge that they need to please God. But even if we do our best to bring them up in the light, there may be things within the child himself that draws him towards the darkness.

- Our responsibility is not to blame ourselves for the child's failure to succeed, but to be a foundation that the child can use to change his ways.
- In other words, we are responsible for providing our child with the tools he needs to please God, but we cannot do it for him because it is up to him to do for himself what God requires of him.

## THE CRY OF THE PROPHET:

David's cry of intense grief for Absalom was a foreshadowing and an illustration of God the Father's sorrow for unsaved people in a world of sin and darkness. David could not die for Absalom. While most fathers would give their lives to save their children, those children must die at some time.

David's cry expresses the heart of God the Father, and that heart desire was fulfilled at the death of Jesus Christ because, through Christ, God found a way to save us from death. And so, David's cry of grief was not only the anguish of a mourning father but also an echo of the anguish of a God who wants to see all of us live eternally.

## CONCLUSION:

The Bible tells us that our highest duty to our children is to love them. Because of that love, we take the time and the energy to equip them to succeed spiritually. Ultimately, we must allow them to live their own lives, but we can establish a Biblical foundation. There is one who has died for our children so that they might have eternal life, and to him be all the glory.

## NOTES:

# Six

# THORN IN THE FLESH

**T**ext: *⁷To keep me from becoming conceited because of these surpassingly great revelations, there was given me a thorn in my flesh, a messenger of Satan, to torment me. ⁸Three times I pleaded with the Lord to take it away from me. ⁹But he said to me, "My grace is sufficient for you, for my power is made perfect in weakness." Therefore I will boast all the more gladly about my weaknesses, so that Christ's power may rest on me. ¹⁰That is why, for Christ's sake, I delight in weaknesses, in insults, in hardships, in persecutions, in difficulties. For when I am weak, then I am strong.* **2 Corinthians 12:7-10 (NIV)**

## INTRODUCTION:

It doesn't take too long after you are saved to realize that you are on a lifelong adventure. Jesus expects you to grow into a mature Christian and a knowledgeable servant. And yet, because of our human nature, almost all of us run into "thorns in our side" that prevented us from maturing into the Christian that Christ wants us to become. The question I intend to answer in this sermon is how do you deal with those obstacles, blockages, disappointments, and frustrations which prevent you from growing and maturing as a Christian?

## MODERN DAY EXAMPLES:

Our culture is technologically more advanced than the culture that Paul experienced. Nevertheless, human nature is still subject to the same "thorns" that Paul suffered. Examples of modern-day thorns are:

- Weaknesses are the same as character faults. These character defects bring suffering and turmoil. They are personality problems that are very difficult to correct and painful to endure.

- Injuries are the same as offenses. Offenses initially bring emotional pain but quickly turn into anger which can evolve into hate. Resolving offenses is an art not readily learned by many of us.
- Necessities are the same as the need for provisions. Poverty is a curse and living in fear of it is even worse.
- Persecutions are the same as social rejections. We can be abused socially by bullies or family members that reject who we are so we can meet their emotional needs. The roles assigned to us can be unfair and damaging.
- Distresses are the same as emotional stresses. Such emotions as anxiety, depression, and anger are common even in the church. Depression is a frequent and widespread complaint of many people.

## PAUL'S THORN:

Paul was not very clear about what kind of thorn he had, and so we don't know what the thorn was, but three ideas have been advanced:

1. A physical disease caught from mission's work. Please note that Paul considered the Devil as the source of illness.
2. Poor eyesight. Paul's thorn tormented him, and poor vision would undoubtedly frustrate and stress Paul in his ministry.
3. Those who came after to discredit his teachings. Paul spoke of "a messenger," and this could be a person or a group of people who were attempting to invalidate his teachings.

Of these three ideas, the second and third are the most likely.

## PAUL'S PRAYER:

Paul would seek the help of the Lord to remove the thorn so Paul could be a more efficient and effective minister of the Gospel. The Lord's response is eye-opening.

- He asked the Lord repeatedly. He prayed three times, and not to get an answer immediately was probably unusual for him
- He specifically asked for the thorn's removal. Depending on what the thorn was, this could be a prayer of either healing or protection.

The Lord answered his prayer, but the answer was not what Paul wanted to hear.

## MY GRACE:

God did answer Paul. The Lord wanted to bring about a change in Paul's attitude, and so the Lord took the following steps:

- Paul wanted to be relieved of his thorn because he saw it as a handicap – a restriction or limitation.
- The Lord saw it as an opportunity to show himself strong.
- The Lord gave Paul a sufficient amount of "unmerited favor" for Paul to overcome the limitations of his "thorn."

## PAUL'S BOASTING:

Paul had a total change in understanding and attitude about his thorn. This new perspective of his thorn was life-changing. This change was of two types:

1. He no longer saw his thorn as a handicap, but as a way to demonstrate the power of Christ.
2. He took this understanding and applied it to all his other weaknesses and handicaps and became victorious over them.

What once was a tormenting handicap now is a source of strength because Paul had a more profound understanding of God's grace. What was meant by Satan to stop Paul was now a reason to spread the good news of God's unmerited favor (grace).

## CONCLUSION:

No matter what area of your life is affected, God's grace is sufficient for you to have the victory. In each weakness is his strength so that each vulnerability can lead to a ministry of his power. Your faults and deficiencies do not cause God to reject you, but when asked he will strengthen and enlighten you about your victory through grace

## NOTES:

# Seven

## DELIVERANCE MINISTRY

**T**ext: *²²Then some people brought to Jesus, a man who was blind and could not talk because he had a demon. Jesus healed the man so that he could talk and see.* **Matthew 12:22 (NCV)**

*¹⁷And those who believe will be able to do these things as proof: They will use my name to force out demons. They will speak in new languages.* **Mark 16:17 (NCV)**

### INTRODUCTION:

Finding a church with a deliverance ministry is rare. If you read any of the gospels, you will see that deliverance ministry was a frequent and essential part of the ministry of Jesus. In each of the gospels, he dealt with both demons and unclean spirits, and people got free from bondage. In our scientifically orientated culture the belief in spirits is considered superstition, and if the church follows the values of our culture, it will reject deliverance ministry or even the reality of spirits. Nevertheless, there is a need for this kind of ministry because people still feel the impact of spirits and spiritual forces that mean to harm them. In this sermon, I intend to describe the deliverance ministry and what it takes to establish such a ministry in the church.

### DEMONS AND UNCLEAN SPIRITS:

There is some scriptural support for the idea that demons are angels that followed Satan and fell along with him. For example, Satan is called the prince of demons and since Satan was a fallen angel one would expect demons to be fallen angels as well.

While the terms unclean spirit and demon are used interchangeably, the emphasis for the unclean spirit is that they represent some form of human behavior that is unholy or which rejects the Word of God. Demons are also unclean, but they seem to be more powerful and aggressive, causing more harm to their victims.

## THE IMPACT OF DEMONS:

Both demons and unclean spirits can affect a person in three ways. The only difference between the demon or unclean spirit is the degree of intensity and frequency of the attacks. A demon is much more capable of disabling its victim in a shorter period. The impacts that these spirits can have on a person are:

- They can influence the person. Influence means that they can suggest a course of action which is sinful or that rejects God.
- They can oppress the person. Oppression is a substantial, continuous, and powerful influence. The person is literally haunted by the demon or unclean spirit.
- They can possess the person. Possession means that the demon has taken over the person's personality and behavior. The demon replaces the person's fundamental values and causes the person to behave destructively, including self-destruction. Born again and Spirit-filled Christians are naturally protect against possession because they are filled with the Spirit of God.

## EXORCISM OR DELIVERANCE:

There are obvious differences between exorcism and deliverance ministry.

- Exorcism uses church ritual and is dependent on pre-written prayers. It also uses such tools as holy water, incense, and crucifixes to dislodge the unclean spirit or demon.
- Deliverance is what Jesus did to cast out a demon or unclean spirit. Jesus stood in his authority as God and through the Holy Spirit's power to commanded the spirits to leave. (Matthew 12:28)
- There is no recorded case in which the spirit was able to disobey Jesus. In most cases, the spirit didn't even attempt to fight Jesus to remain in its victim.

Either method can work, but most Spirit-filled Christians will desire to work along with the Holy Spirit.

As a result, Christians with a deliverance ministry must stand in the authority of Christ. No demon or unclean spirit can resist a command to leave given in the name of Jesus Christ.

## WHAT IS NEEDED:

The Baptism of the Holy Spirit is empowering and vital to deliverance. Deliverance does not take place just because someone is using the name of Jesus. Deliverance takes place because the power of the Holy Spirit is released and no demon or unclean spirit can stand against it.

One of the gifts of the Holy Spirit is discernment. This means that the people involved with deliverance ministry must discern what is going on before attempting deliverance. There are alternatives to the intrusion of spirits such as:

- Mental illness.
- Pseudo-possession.
- Attention-getting.
- Religious delusion.

All these factors can play a role in deliverance ministry, and it is necessary for the people who are conducting the deliverance service to know what is going on. The Holy Spirit can also impart the gifts of wisdom and knowledge. Both these gifts will not only help in deliverance, but they will also enable the deliverance minister to know how to pray and how to command the spirit to depart from its victim.

The final thing needed by a deliverance ministry is training. The training is of several types:

- Training about Scriptures is necessary to build the confidence and faith of the people involved in deliverance.
- Training is needed in teamwork. Teams are much better for this ministry than sole individuals because team members can support each other.
- Training is needed in basic abnormal psychology. Such training can help deal with mental issues after deliverance has taken place.

## CONCLUSION:

Deliverance ministry is not for every church. If such a ministry is desired, every precaution must be taken to keep it balanced with Scripture and common sense. Train before you attempt to deliver, and be sure to have follow-up available for those delivered. Be sure to establish a healthy team ministry that is willing to give of their time and resources to make the ministry efficient. Listen to the Holy Spirit before you act, but when you move have confidence in Jesus. Remember that the Devil cannot stand against you if you have the Holy Spirit with you.

## NOTES:

# *Eight*

# FAITH FOR TOMORROW

**T**ext: *⁵ Trust the LORD with all your heart, and don't depend on your own understanding. ⁶ Remember the LORD in all you do, and he will give you success. ⁷Don't depend on your own wisdom. Respect the LORD and refuse to do wrong. ⁸Then your body will be healthy, and your bones will be strong.* **Proverbs 3:5-8 (NCV)**

## INTRODUCTION:

Some of the older people here may remember that as a child in elementary school, they used to have drills in which they would hide underneath their school chairs. We tried to protect ourselves from the Russians dropping nuclear weapons on our cities. We lived in fear of the future, an emotion exceeded by the fear of the future in which we now live. We must also come to understand the fact that the older we get, the more uncertain we become about the future and the more fearful that future becomes. We all share a time in life where the future was exciting and something we looked forward to with joy. The Bible instructs us about how to live without fear of the future. The verse which is our text today gives us some basic principles which we can implement to have faith in tomorrow.

Vs. 5: *⁵ Trust the LORD with all your heart, and don't depend on your own understanding.*

This verse states that we are to trust the Lord with all our heart, but that is easier said than done for most of us.

- Trusting the Lord with all your heart can become a stumbling block because the Bible references the heart as the place of our emotions, and often, our heart is confused and unstable.
- What this essentially means is that we need to replace fear of the future with trust in the Lord.
- The conflict then is between the emotions based on a trust in God and the feelings generated by our judgment or understanding of our possible future.
- Our analysis of what may happen in the future may have nothing to do with God's plan for us. If we base our emotions on our analysis, we ignore God's plan. The result is suffering and fear of the future.
- Even if the future is dark and full of suffering, if we know and trust God and his plan for us, we can endure and move through the future maintaining peace within our hearts.

Vs. 6: *⁶Remember the LORD in all you do, and he will give you success.*

We are taught to be independent and self-directed individuals. As a result, it's difficult for us to allow God to lead us. We must also realize that there are insurmountable mountains on the path we would like to travel in the future. Conquering those mountains by ourselves is a hopeless task.

- This Scripture says that we are to follow God. That means we are to involve him and obey him in every turn of events.
- Our tendency, because we are trained to be "adults" who are to make adult decisions, is to either ignore or reject God's will in our lives.
- If we are to follow God, then we must reject the tendency to ignore him by giving him a priority in the decisions that we make.
- The second part of the Scripture is a promise. This promise is that God will remove those insurmountable obstacles, those unmovable mountains which block our path. So, we must remember that with God, all things are possible.

Vs. 7: *⁷Don't depend on your own wisdom. Respect the LORD and refuse to do wrong.*

Jerome A. Jochem M.S., M.A.

The lack of recognition of our limitations results in a lack of faith in the future, and so we make incorrect and foolish decisions which eventually hurt us and make us fearful.

- Without consulting God in our decision-making process, we continually make mistakes which produce more uncertainty and fear about our future.
- When we were young, we were also both ignorant and inexperienced, and we paid the consequences as we grew older.
- As we grow older, there is less confidence in our decisions. Our past mistakes haunt us.
- It is not until we conclude that we are not equipped to make all decisions by ourselves that we can start making decisions based on God's plan. In other words, we must learn to respect God and his wisdom in guiding us into the future.
- Once we have learned to respect God, we include him in our decisions and move according to his will, and that produces a positive future.
- The only thing that would inhibit this process of including God in our decisions is a lifestyle of sin and evil. Evil will always result in a negative, unhappy, and painful future.

Vs. 8: *8Then your body will be healthy, and your bones will be strong.*

Verse 8 ends this Scripture portion with a promise. That is if you develop faith in God for the future, then your future will be healthy and you will feel strong both physically and in terms of your faith.

- Verse eight assumes that you are no longer in conflict with God's will, that you are trusting your future to him, that you believe he is with you always, that his plan for you is good and will result in a future which once again is exciting and filled with hope.
- One can only implement the principles in the initial verses and wait and see what the consequences are going to be regarding your health and strength.
- God does not lie or make empty promises.

## CONCLUSION:

In a world which continually predicts darkness and suffering for the future, it is a great blessing to find peace and confidence because you are following God who is leading you through your future. This is worthwhile having and a great blessing. Let us, therefore, trust God, allow him to guide us, subject our barriers and mountains to his will, and be at peace in the present about the future. Remember, that the best of all prospects is the one that God has chosen for you, and he will make a way when there seems to be no way.

## NOTES:

# *Nine*

# FIVE PRINCIPLES OF
# GREAT WORSHIP.

**T**ext: *²³Yet a time is coming and has now come when the true worshipers will worship the Father in spirit and truth, for they are the kind of worshipers the Father seeks. ²⁴ God is spirit, and his worshipers must worship in spirit and in truth.* **John 4:23-24 (NIV)**

*⁴ For everything that was written in the past was written to teach us, so that through endurance and the encouragement of the Scriptures we might have hope.* **Romans 15:4 (NIV)**

## INTRODUCTION:

As Christians, we know that the Holy Spirit will guide us to worship God. Our text tells us that God is Spirit and we must worship him in spirit and truth. So, the Holy Spirit will enable our worship, but what is the reality of worship? Where do we find the truth about how to worship? Well, the only truth that we have is in the Bible, so we must base worship on the commands and descriptions of worship found in the Bible. That includes what is mentioned in the Old Testament, but not repeated in the New Testament. Concerning the Old Testament, remember what Paul said in Romans 15:4, and understand that the prescribed methods of worship found in the Old Testament are relevant today.

I would like to outline five basic principles which will ensure powerful and life-changing worship:

## THE FIVE PRINCIPLES:
### 1). Be a Participator, not a Spectator

The Bible tells us of several ways that we can participate in praise and worship:

- Singing.

*4 Sing praises to the LORD, you who belong to him; praise his holy name.* **Psalms 30:4 (NCV)**

*1Sing to the LORD a new song, sing to the LORD, all the earth 2 Sing to the LORD and praise his name; every day tell how he saves us.* **Psalms 96:1-2 (NCV)**

- Kneeling/Bowing.

*6 Come, let us bow down in worship, let us kneel before the LORD our Maker; 7 for he is our God and we are the people of his pasture, the flock under his care.* **Psalm 95:6-7 (NIV)**

- Lifting Hands.

*2 Lift up your hands in the sanctuary and praise the LORD.* **Psalm 134:2 (NIV)**

*8 I want men everywhere to lift up holy hands in prayer, without anger or disputing.* **1 Timothy 2:8 (NIV)**

- Clapping Hands/Shouting.

*1 Clap your hands, all you nations; shout to God with cries of joy.* **Psalm 47:1 (NIV)**

- Dancing/ Musical Instruments.

*3 Let them praise his name with dancing and make music to him with tambourine and harp.* **Psalm 149:3 (NIV)**

*3 Praise him with the sounding of the trumpet, praise him with the harp and lyre, 4 praise him with tambourine and dancing, praise him with the strings and flute,5 praise him with the clash of cymbals, praise him with resounding cymbals.* **Psalm 150:3-5 (NIV)**

- Singing a "New Song"

*1 Praise the LORD! Sing a new song to the LORD; sing his praise in the meeting of his people.* **Psalm 149:1 (NCV)**

*9And they all sang a new song to the Lamb.* **Revelation 5:9 (NCV)**

## 2). Be Free:

The Bible gives you the freedom to praise and worship the Lord in all the ways that I just listed. If you do not practice that freedom, your worship and praise will be severely restricted by several personal factors:

- Fear that someone will criticize you, or shame you, or judge you for your form of worship.
- Insecurity because you feel you can't worship well in song or dance or any other style.
- Guilt, produced by false teaching about praise and worship.

## 3). Content:

By content, I mean what you are feeling and saying to God as you worship. This is a direct measure of how well you are relating to God during worship.

- Don't confuse style with content. The style is how you worship not how well you worship.
- You can choose any style you feel most comfortable with, but the content must always be focused on God and God only.
- If you begin to worship the style of the song, you have entered the realm of entertainment and not worship.

## 4). To Break Through, Break Out:

There are times when worship will flow smoothly, and you will enter the glory quickly and with no distractions. At other times, you may be easily distracted, and find little reason or motivation to worship.

- When worship seems to be the very last thing you want to do, you have the opportunity to offer God a sacrifice of praise. [15] *Through Jesus, therefore, let us continually offer to God a sacrifice of praise--the fruit of lips that confess his name.* **Hebrews 13:15 (NIV)**
- The sacrifice of praise is made with our mouths, that is, it must be spoken out loud, even in the most challenging situations, and we praise whether we feel like doing it or not.

## 5). Expect His Glory.

*[3]Yet you are enthroned as the Holy One; you are the praise of Israel.* **Psalm 22:3 (NIV)**

This Scripture implies that God dwells and is exalted in the praises of his people. He is the God surrounded by holiness, love, and glory. As we worship him, we should expect to experience by revelation, the Glory of God.

## CONCLUSION:

The outcome of worship is something beautiful which fills our hearts. We join our hearts to God, and his life and love flow into our spirits and souls. We know that we are his children and he is ever more our Father God. As his children, we can receive during worship, his healing, peace, and love as well as the other fruit of the Spirit. If we do nothing else when we meet, let us worship him with a heart full of thanksgiving and gratitude.

## NOTES:

# Ten

# BURDENS

**T**ext: *30For my yoke is easy and my burden is light."* **Matthew 11:30(NIV)**

*You teachers are also in for trouble! You load people down with heavy burdens, but you won't lift a finger to help them carry the loads.* **Luke 11:46 (NCV)**

## INTRODUCTION:

In our text for today, the word 'burden" means a task or duty to perform. Jesus said that God will give believers burdens but that his burdens are light. What he meant was that the tasks he gives us are not impossible to do. With his help, we can accomplish these burdens, and they are always for the benefit of ourselves or others. The second Scripture is an admonishment to the teachers of the law who demanded that people do the impossible, but they will not help in any way. Such burdens are called "heavy," implying that they are challenging and hard to accomplish resulting in constant failure. In this sermon, I intend to draw distinctions between the Lord's burdens and heavy burdens so that we can eliminate the heavy loads and fulfill the light ones.

## CHARACTERISTICS OF HEAVY BURDENS:

All heavy burdens tend to share the same characteristics regardless of the exact nature of the task. A few of the features of heavy burdens are:

- Heavy burdens are generally religious. They include such things as following legalistic laws that govern what you do, what you wear, how you think, and how you treat others who are different from you.

- Regardless of how religious they appear, heavy burdens originate from Satan. The Devil wants to load you down with unnecessary, wasteful, and discouraging tasks. The more time you spend trying to do the impossible and the worse you feel when you fail, the better Satan likes it.
- You spend so much time and energy trying to carry out a heavy burden that you are not fruitful in other more critical areas in your spiritual life.
- Every time you fail at completing the heavy burden, the burden gets heavier. You find that after you fail you must deal with your failure and that makes the task even more impossible.
- No one, including the Devil, will help you finish the task and so the heavy burden is constant and without relief.
- The only way to cast-off a heavy burden is to fight it and reject it through a form of spiritual warfare. You must depend on Christ to set you free!
- Since heavy burdens originate from the Devil, they have long-term effects such as stealing your peace, destroying your faith, and killing your relationship with God by diminishing your love for him.

To eliminate a heavy burden, a person must recognize it for what it is. Must see that it is detrimental to a healthy spiritual life, and make an effort to reject it in preference to the light burdens of Christ.

## LIGHT BURDENS OF THE LORD:

The Lord said that he would give us burdens, but his burdens are not hard to bear and are accomplished successfully with the help of the Holy Spirit. The Lord's burdens also share some characteristics such as:

- The Lord's burdens tend to be spiritual. They involve such tasks as praying, ministering, and giving support to others for the common good.
- The Holy Spirit controls the Lord's burdens, and such a burden may be intensified to the degree that there is a strong urge to complete it. The burden may seem to be spiritually critical, and the need to finish it is dominant and overbearing.
- The Lord's burdens produce spiritual growth because the Holy Spirit equips and enables the believer.

- These types of burdens also reinforce submission and obedience to God.
- Once accomplished, the burden is gone. It is lifted from the believer. The Holy Spirit either tells the believer that the burden is ended, or relieves the requirement to obey and submit because the burden is completed.
- The believer's awareness of God has expanded, and the believer wants to be of additional service to the Lord.
- In the future, the believer will more readily tell the difference between a heavy burden and a burden from the Lord.
- The long-term effects of the Lord's burdens include increased spiritual awareness of God, stronger ministry, and a more profound understanding of the believer's service to God.

God has given us burdens, but those burdens center around love. The Holy Spirit will help us to love others by helping us to complete the Lord's burdens.

## CONCLUSION:

The next time you feel a burden to pray or intercede for someone, don't resist but be obedient and do what the Lord wants, The Holy Spirit has given you a responsibility to help someone and to bless someone who may be desperately needing your aid. Be submitted to the burden and accomplish what the Lord intended by giving it to you in the first place. It may feel like a burden, but it is also a blessing.

## NOTES:

*Eleven*

# POWERFUL PRAYER

**T**ext: [19]*"Also, I tell you that if two of you on earth agree about something and pray for it, it will be done for you by my Father in heaven.* [20]*This is true because if two or three people come together in my name, I am there with them."* **Matthew 18:19-20(NCV)**

[22]*Jesus answered,"Have faith in God.* [23]*I tell you the truth, you can say to this mountain, 'Go, fall into the sea.' And if you have no doubts in your mind and believe that what you say will happen, God will do it for you.* [24]*So I tell you to believe that you have received the things you ask for in prayer, and God will give them to you.* [25]*When you are praying, if you are angry with someone, forgive him so that your Father in heaven will also forgive your sins."* **Mark 11:22-25 (NCV)**

## INTRODUCTION:

Without a doubt, prayer is one of the most potent weapons in our warfare against the Devil and his kingdom. Many Christians feel challenged about their prayer life because they either do not pray at all or are unsure if they are praying correctly. In this sermon, I would like to discuss some of the issues that surround prayer and encourage us all to pray with power.

**When to pray:** [18]*Pray in the Spirit at all times with all kinds of prayers, asking for everything you need. To do this you must always be ready and never give up. Always pray for all God's people.* **Ephesians 6:18 (NCV)**

Praying is not limited to pre-written prayers, spontaneous prayers, or praying just during church. We should pray without limiting how or when we are to pray.

- Praying spontaneously means that we did not pre-plan when we pray. Often this means we pray according to need and the situation demanding prayer.
- Praying in the Spirit means that we pray through the Holy Spirit to God who hears and understands our prayer. Such prayer may be said using the spiritual gift of tongues if the Christian is baptized in the Holy Spirit.
- Prayers may be written and used as part of a church ritual. Such prayers are often beautiful and poetic. These types of prayers are recited as a congregation during a church service, and so are known as congregational prayers.
- People who pray need to make a time to pray if they want to pray consistently and with perseverance. Just because God may not answer immediately is not a reason to stop praying.

**How to pray:** [7]*"And when you pray, don't be like those people who don't know God. They continue saying things that mean nothing, thinking that God will hear them because of their many words.* [8]*Don't be like them, because your Father knows the things you need before you ask him* **Matthew 6:7-8 (NCV)**

[56]*When you pray, you should go into your room and close the door and pray to your Father who cannot be seen. Your Father can see what is done in secret, and he will reward you.* **Matthew 6:56 (NCV)**

- Powerful prayer is not so much about what you say as it is about the passion behind the prayer.
- Using a lot of words to generate a long prayer does not guarantee that God hears your prayer. Also, prayers that repeat phrases and words are not necessarily efficient or powerful.
- Since God already knows what we need, our prayers can be simple requests, petitions, and pleas to God for an answer.
- Do not be afraid to express yourself emotionally. God is not put off by feelings, and Jesus, because he was fully human, understands and has empathy for your emotions.

## ANSWERS TO PRAYER:

God does answer prayers, and you can expect an answer to your prayer as well. The way that he answers prayer varies, and you must be aware of how he may respond to your prayers. He has answered prayers in the following ways;

- Answer withheld: Jesus asked that his cup of suffering be taken away, but submitted to his Fathers will instead. (Matthew 26:39). In the same way, our prayers may not be answered as we would like.

- Answer delayed: God may not immediately answer prayer. He may wait for the right time, place, or condition to answer prayer. Patience is required with faith that he will answer.

- Answer exceeds: When Peter was in jail, the disciples prayed for him. He was miraculously delivered from the Roman prison, an outcome that exceeded expectations. (Acts 12:16).

- Answer different than request: Paul requested that God remove the thorn in his flesh. Instead, God told him that grace was sufficient. (2 Corinthians 12: 7ff)

- Answer promised: The answer to our prayers comes at the will of God. Because we can trust him to answer, we can believe in his promises. (Hebrews 10:23)

- The answer is given: The Bible is full of stories where God answered prayer. In fact, both in the Old and New Testaments significant prayers were responded to for around 35 different people.

**Faith and Prayer**: *[24]So I tell you to believe that you have received the things you ask for in prayer, and God will give them to you.[25]When you are praying, if you are angry with someone, forgive him so that your Father in heaven will also forgive your sins.* **Mark 11:24-25 (NCV)**

Faith is a requirement if you want your prayers answered. Keep in mind the following factors before you begin to pray. These factors are vital if your faith is weak or unstable.

- Why would you ask God for something for yourself or others if you do not believe that your prayer will be answered in some way?
- You may have to build your hope before you pray. Hope energizes prayer when facing a hopeless situation.

- You may have to strengthen your faith by preparing your heart to pray before you say your prayer. Such heart preparations can take place by:
    - o Reading the Word and the promises of God.
    - o By remembering that God answered your prayers in the past.
    - o Giving thanks to him for his goodness and love for you and the person for whom you are praying.
    - o Worshipping God and by doing so, coming into his presence through the Holy Spirit.
    - o Forgiving those who offended you.

**Mistakes in Prayer:** [5]*"When you pray, don't be like the hypocrites. They love to stand in the synagogues and on the street corners and pray so people will see them. I tell you the truth, they already have their full reward.* **Matthew 6:5 (NCV)**

Praying in public carries with it some warnings and traps. Make sure you are focused on God and not trying to impress the people around you. God does not require a public appearance to answer our prayers.

- Check your motivations for praying. Are you praying for human consumption or are you praying to touch the heart of God?
- If you find yourself praying to impress people, then you should stop and re-direct your prayer to God. If you continue to pray to look good before other Christians, their admiration will be your reward. Ask yourself, is that what you desire or do you want to talk to God?

## CONCLUSION:

If we understand the fundamental principles concerning passionate and dynamic prayer, we are well on our way to victory over the work of the Devil impacting our lives. We need to talk to Jesus about everything and at all times. He is with us every day, and he hears us and will respond. Be encouraged and keep on praying with determination and perseverance. God loves you and will answer, and his answer is always for your best possible future.

NOTES:

# OVERCOMING DISCOURAGEMENT

**T**ext*: Why, my soul, are you downcast? Why so disturbed within me? Put your hope in God, for I will yet praise him, my Savior and my God.* (**Palms. 42:5**)

## INTRODUCTION:

Every single person that I know has had to face discouragement. Some of those people become so discouraged that they gave up, on their jobs, on their children, and on their marriage. Why do we as human beings become so discouraged that we give up? Why is it that Christians, even though they know the Lord Jesus Christ, can become so discouraged that they stop walking in the Spirit and fall back into the world? Let us consider the following:

## BY FAITH NOT SIGHT:

In 2 Corinthians the Bible states *"For we walk by faith, not by sight"* This means we do not explicitly see our Christian voyage. **2 Corinthians. 5:7 (NCV)**

- There is no question that we want to find our direction in life by using what we would call common sense. We want a clear and precise understanding of what the next step will bring as we walk through life.
- What this Scripture is saying is that God's plan may not be our plan and that we may not comprehend what he has in mind for us.
- We want to be in control and have a clear path to our goals and objectives in life, and often, a part of us rebels against what God wants for us. The result is discouragement because we fail,

flounder, and stumble through life all the while trying to make everything work for us the way we want it to work out.

- To overcome that discouragement, we must realize that God has a plan for us and trust him to help us through. Scripture gives us the antidote for this discouragement when it says: *⁵ Trust the LORD with all your heart, and don't depend on your own understanding.* **Proverbs 3:5 (NCV)**
- So, we must walk by faith into the mysterious future that God has for us, and even when we do not understand, trust he will always give us a blessing. This takes courage and determination, but the end is well rewarded because of our obedience.

## TEAM WORK:
When God tells us to do something, we may have to work along with others. From the nature of the Trinity to the descriptions of Jesus working with his disciples, we can see that God is a team player and wants us to be a member of his team.

- Within all of us, there are weaknesses which can lead to discouragement as members of God's team.
- For example, if you don't trust the other members of your church, or you are afraid of conflict with them, then you will become discouraged because you cannot accomplish the goals that God wants you to achieve as a member of a team.
- Some weaknesses revolve around personality differences; you may get discouraged because you feel that someone in your church does not like you or make it clear that they do not want to work with you.

The solution to this discouragement is found in the Lord's command to love each other. Love indeed covers a multitude of offenses and enables us to work as one. The more you learn to love, the better you will work as a team.

## WALK ON WATER:
It may seem that God is asking us to do the impossible. When we realize the difficulty of what he is asking of us, we may become discouraged and despondent.

- For example, if there is someone in your life that hurt you, abused you, damaged you, and made your life like hell, God may ask you to forgive that person.
- Such forgiveness may seem impossible, and way beyond what your anger calls for you to do. You may be right; it may be impossible for you on your own to forgive that person for his sins against you that brought you so much pain and suffering. All that means is that you need God to help you forgive the unforgivable.
- Another cause of discouragement may be that God is asking you to do something that is way beyond your abilities. Something that no amount of education or training will prepare you to do. As we recognize our own limitations, we become discouraged.

The solution to these sources of discouragement is the same. You are to cast yourself upon the Lord and ask him to help you to do want he wants, and to provide the resources to accomplish his will in your life. Look to him and not yourself because [26]*Jesus looked at them and said,"This is something people cannot do, but God can do all things."* **Matthew 19:26 (NCV)**

## OUR OPPOSITION:

You do not need to be a great, famous, or well-known Christian for Satan to oppose you and your walk with the Lord. Satan opposes all of us because our walk is a testimony about Christ, and if Satan can discourage you then your testimony is weakened.

Satan will discourage you in every area of your life. He will bring about:
- Financial discouragement. (Not enough money, but too many bills.)
- Emotional discouragement. (Depression, anxiety, fear.)
- Physical discouragement. (Sickness and disease.)
- Relational discouragement. (Hatred and offense.)
- Spiritual discouragement. (Failure and discontent.)

Perhaps the single most important understanding that will help you defeat Satan's discouragement is the knowledge that Christ has already won the war and that Satan is the loser, not you. Discouragement is overcome when the believer recognizes victory.

## CONCLUSION

In every situation of discouragement that I discussed here, the solution is to put your faith, trust, obedience, and perseverance in the Lord. Jesus will change your despair to victory and joy as you follow him throughout your life. Just remember to take your hope from the one who cares for you.

## NOTES:

# THE SHIELD OF FAITH

**T**ext:[16]*And also use the shield of faith with which you can stop all the burning arrows of the Evil One.* **Ephesians 6:16 (NCV)**

## INTRODUCTION:

It is a common and truthful observation that the Devil frequently attacks Christians. He aims at those serving God to expand God's kingdom, and not only attacks these individuals but will also attack family members and friends. Satan's attacks take several forms ranging from financial trouble to sickness. These "burning arrows' seem to come from external sources, are unexpected, and may destroy or even kill those afflicted. One of our primary defenses against the attacks of the Devil is our shield of faith, and in this sermon, I would like to explore why our shield is a robust defense against the Devil's attacks.

## WHAT KIND OF FAITH:

While faith has many forms and expressions, we can simplify our understanding of faith by reducing it to three kinds:

1. Faith that God exists. The belief that God exists is foundational to warfare against the Devil. The Devil's attacks are supernatural and negative. His attacks are countered and defeated by God who is also supernatural and positive. Without trust in God, we have no defense.
2. Faith that God is involved in our lives. It is not enough just to believe in God; we must also know that he is involved in our lives and knows when we suffer from an attack by the Devil. Trusting

that God cares about us, is the handle by which we hold on to our shield.

3. Faith that all of God's promises are true. If God is a liar, then we have no basis to believe that he has given us a shield. If God does not keep his promises to us, then we have no protection and will remain victims of the hate of the Devil.

## HOW THE SHIELD WORKS:

How does the shield of faith act to stop the attacks of the Devil? The shield works in two primary ways to protect us from the burning arrows:

1. The shield acts as a barrier and so prevents the attacks from doing severe damage to ourselves or those who we love. Because of our faith, we can live in victory even if the Devil has knocked us off our feet with some bad news. Our shield is a defense from the most destructive aspects of the attack.

2. It quenches the arrows making them useless, and so the attack loses its power to destroy us. The shield of faith prevents us from doubting God and by doing so making the attack more severe. Our shield of faith helps us to victory even in the most catastrophic assualts of Satan.

## MAINTAINING THE SHIELD:

At the time of Christ, a shield was made of wood and covered in leather sealed with metal edges. We maintain our shield by preserving our faith and through Scripture:

• Faith keeps the leather from cracking. Scripture tells us that Christ is our strength and defense. Scripture supports our faith so that we can believe regardless of the nature of the attack.

• By soaking the shield in the rivers of living water that Jesus promises to believers.

[38]*If anyone believes in me, rivers of living water will flow out from that person's heart, as the Scripture says."* **John 7:38 (NCV)** Soaking the shield with the living water from Christ means allowing the Holy Spirit to infuse faith with power, A power to defeat the power of the enemy because the power of the Holy Spirit is far superior to the power of the evil one.

Jerome A. Jochem M.S., M.A.

## THE TRUE NATURE OF THE SHIELD:

*¹After these things happened, the LORD spoke his word to Abram in a vision: "Abram, don't be afraid. I will defend you, and I will give you a great reward."* **Genesis 15:1 (NCV)**

We tend to think of our shield as an object, but it is our relationship with God that is our real shield.

- The foundation of that relationship is love. The realization of God's love for us gives us confidence that he will defend us against an enemy more powerful than anyone other than God.
- As we depend on God to defend us, our faith in God deepens. Our growing belief makes our shield stronger.
- As our shield becomes strong, the Devil's attacks will become impotent. That does not mean that the Devil will stop attacking, but his attacks will not damage us as the Devil intended.

## CONCLUSION:

The shield of faith is a piece of spiritual armor that we must activate for it to protect us. The attacks of the devil are constant, so the shield must be used consistently. Like Abraham, when we build our relationship with God, our faith grows, and our shield becomes stronger. Reading the Word and allowing the Holy Spirit to empower will all contribute to having a healthy shield of faith.

## NOTES:

# THE MANIFEST PRESENCE OF GOD

T**ext:** [21] *Those who know my commands and obey them are the ones who love me, and my Father will love those who love me. I will love them and will show myself to them.* " **John 14:21 (NCV)**

[2] *To the church of God in Corinth, to you who have been made holy in Christ Jesus. You were called to be God's holy people with all people everywhere who pray in the name of the Lord Jesus Christ—their Lord and ours.* **1 Corinthians 1:2 (NCV)**

## INTRODUCTION:

The goal of the walk that we have with the Holy Spirit is to develop an intense and close relationship with our Lord Jesus. Such secondary goals as ministry, service, and even worship play a role in our walk, but they are not the ultimate personal purpose. Every Christian should be driven by the desire for unity with Christ. Such a union is the ultimate destiny of all Christians, but it is difficult to both understand and achieve this type of communion. The purpose of this sermon is to give at least a basic understanding of how to achieve this closeness based on the character of God, particularly his love and his holiness.

## THE MANIFEST PRESENCE:

As the name implies, the manifest presence is how Jesus shows himself to us through the Holy Spirit. Instances of the manifest presence are:

- An extremely powerful sense of the presence of the Holy Spirit and glory of God
- Being physically overwhelmed to the degree that we are swept off our feet.

- Individual visions and prophetic statements flow easily.
- Having what recently is called the "holy laughter."
- Physical manifestation such as the gold or silver dust appearing on people and inanimate objects.
- Both physical and mental supernatural healings.
- Working of miracles, that is, events which transcend the laws of physics.

## THE PROBLEM:

While the manifest presence allows people to experience the power of God in operation, it does not reveal the individual personality or the nature of God. Take for example the following:

- If the light is manifested, the light is not God, but God is producing light.
- If the holy laughter occurs, the laughter is not God, but God is bringing about the laughter.
- If the laws of the cosmos are transcended, the laws of the universe are not God, but God created the laws.

The point I'm trying to make is that behind the manifestation of God is the nature and character of God. We must look through or beyond the manifestation to see the divine person producing the manifestation. What must be imperative for us is to break through the manifestation and acknowledge the purposes of God. We must find union and unity with the person causing the manifestation. So, two conditions must be implemented:

## THE FIRST CONDITION IS LOVE:

Before union with Christ can be achieved or is even possible, there must be great love and passion for Christ.

- We show that love and passion for Christ by keeping his commandments the first of which is to love God.
- What that means is that we prioritize God above all things so that he becomes the center of our universe.
- We are asked to express this love of God through obedience, service, and love for others.
- In other words, the primary qualification for union with Christ is that we love him and others as he loved them.

- Without this love found in his two commandments, union with Christ is not remotely possible.

## THE SECOND CONDITION IS HOLINESS:

*:14 Try to live in peace with all people, and try to live free from sin. Anyone whose life is not holy will never see the Lord.* **Hebrews 12:14 (NCV)**

*:4 Everyone will respect you, Lord, and will honor you. Only you are holy. All the nations will come and worship you, because the right things you have done are now made known.* **Revelation 15:4 (NCV)**

We must understand that only God is holy!

As Paul said, we all have fallen short of the mark, and therefore none of us can boast of our holiness. Because of our lack of holiness, it would seem impossible to have any union with the Lord Jesus Christ.

- To solve this problem, Jesus died on the cross for us and by doing so imparted his holiness to us, so that our state of holiness goes from nonexistent to being fully accepted by God.
- Nevertheless, we are still required to live lives free from the sin of the world. In other words, we are to live holy lives: *1 Dear friends, we have these promises from God, so we should make ourselves pure—free from anything that makes body or soul unclean. We should try to become holy in the way we live, because we respect God.* **2 Corinthians 7:1 (NCV)**
- Living a holy life becomes a prerequisite for union with Christ. *15 But be holy in all you do, just as God, the One who called you, is holy. 16 It is written in the Scriptures: "You must be holy because I am holy. "* **1 Peter 1:15-16 (NCV**
- The Holy Spirit helps us to live holy lives by convicting us of our sin, and by reminding us that through the blood of the lamb all sins can be forgiven and our lives restored to a state of holiness.
- To look through the manifest presence and obtain union with Christ, we must withdraw from the entrapment of the world, and when we failed to do that, we must draw upon the sacrifice of Christ.

Jerome A. Jochem M.S., M.A.

## CONCLUSION:

I love, and I am fascinated by the manifest presence of the Lord Jesus Christ through the Holy Spirit. As long as the form of expression is Biblical, I am captivated by the manifestations and desire to experience more of them. We must realize that the manifestations have their limits in that they don't satisfy that deep-rooted hunger for union with Christ. By union, I mean the intimate relationship in which Christ becomes the center of my universe and my all in all. It is vital that we look beyond the manifestations into the heart of God, and that we seek to know him as a person more than as a manifestation of glory.

## NOTES:

# THE PROGRESSION OF
# BIBLICAL HEALING

I NTRODUCTION:
Instead of beginning this sermon with a Scripture reference, I would rather start with a question. The question is, do you believe that God heals today? While many modern-day Christians, especially in the Pentecostal church, believe in divine healing, there are more that do not believe in healing because they have rejected the Baptism of the Holy Spirit. They do not know how to activate the healing gifts and, therefore, have developed doubts that God still heals today. In this sermon, I'd like to show the progression from the Old Testament to the New Testament of the healing ministry, finishing with an explanation of the fact that God does heal today.

## THE OLD TESTAMENT DECLARATIONS:
God the Father's declaration:

The following Scripture reveals God's intent to heal and to be known as a healer.

*I am the LORD who heals you.* (**Exodus 15:26 NCV**)
- God is Jehovah-*rophe*. This name means "Jehovah heals." His name defines his nature and his character as well as his desire to heal.
- God wants to heal and wants to be known as the Great Physician.
- This includes individual as well as national restoration to health.

- It's obvious that God does not bring disease or illness to anyone. It is sin in some shape or form that opens the door to illness. Disease of all types is Satan's work, not God's work.
- Although God will allow us to experience disease because of personal sin, we also experience disease because we live in a fallen world even though personal sin is not involved.

God gave himself this name to encourage us to turn to him when we are attacked with the disease

*David's Declaration*:
³ *He heals the brokenhearted and bandages their wounds.* **Psalms 147:3 (NCV)**

In this psalm, we see David expanding God's healing beyond physical disease.

- The reference to the heart in this psalm is a reference to emotions and mental states.
- The "broken-hearted" are those suffering from both emotional diseases such as anxiety and depression and their correlated physical symptoms.
- According to this psalm, David stated that God's healing is not just for physical disease, but also is designed to heal various types of emotional problems. So, we can conclude that there are at least two significant forms of healing available through God.

*Isaiah's Prophetic Declaration*:
⁴*But he took our suffering on him and felt our pain for us. We saw his suffering and thought God was punishing him.* ⁵ *But he was wounded for the wrong we did; he was crushed for the evil we did. The punishment, which made us well, was given to him, and we are healed because of his wounds.* **Isaiah 53:4-5 (NCV)**

In Isaiah's prophetic declaration we see for the first time a transfer of healing from God the Father to God the Son.

- This prophetic declaration correlates spiritual and physical healing to the redemption found in the suffering servant who is Jesus Christ.

- Healing then is tied to salvation. In the Greek, the word "Sozo" which is used to describe salvation is also used to describe healing.
- Healing has now progressed to include physical, mental, and spiritual dimensions.

## THE NEW TESTAMENT DECLARATIONS:

In the New Testament, we see the healing ministry of God extended through Jesus. Before it was God healing directly through the work of his Spirit, but now in the New Testament, we see Jesus laying hands on people and in a very human-like manner producing healings. So, healing has undergone a progression from God the Father to God the Son.

## THE WORK OF CHRIST:

*35Jesus went through all the towns and villages, teaching in their synagogues, preaching the good news of the kingdom and healing every disease and sickness.* **Matthew 9:35 (NIV)**

Note the three forms of ministry that Jesus undertook while he was in Israel
1. Teaching.
2. Preaching.
3. Healing.

There is no reason to believe that the ministry of Jesus has changed. There is still teaching, preaching in the church, and, through the Holy Spirit, healing should also be taking place.

Pay particular attention to the Scripture where it says that Jesus went about healing "every" disease and sickness. This implies there were no limits to the healing ministry of Jesus.

## THE COMMISSIONING OF THE APOSTLES:

*1He called his 12 disciples to him and gave them authority to drive out evil spirits and to heal every disease and sickness.* **Matthew 10:1 (NIV)**

So far, we have seen the progression of healing from God the Father to God the Son. In this Scripture, Jesus takes that progression one more step by authorizing his followers to heal.

- It is interesting to note that the first transfer of genuine spiritual authority and power from Jesus concerned healing.
- This is very significant because this progression was from God to regular human beings who are now empowered to bring about healing for "every" disease and sickness. This implies that the unlimited authority and the power of Christ got transferred to his apostles.
- Note the mention of spiritual healing in the form of driving out unclean, evil, and demonic spirits. Jesus was not only authorizing his apostles to conduct healing of physical or mental, problems, but also the deliverance from spiritual illness caused by outside demonic influences.

## THE FINAL PROGRESSION:

*7 now to each one the manifestation of the Spirit is given for the common good. 8 To one there is given through the Spirit the message of wisdom, to another the message of knowledge by means of the same Spirit, 9 to another faith by the same Spirit, to another gifts of healing by that one Spirit.* 1 **Corinthians 12:7–9 (NIV)**

Scripture defines the state of healing as it should exist in the church today.

- Healing progressed from God the Father to God the Son, and then from God the Son to his apostles, and, in this Scripture, from God the Holy Spirit to every Christian who has received the Baptism of the Holy Spirit.
- The phrase *"gifts of healing"* is plural. This is not just one type of healing gift but all types required to heal physical, mental, and spiritual diseases.
- The minister will receive the appropriate gift according to the individualized needs of the person asking for healing.
- There is no implication here that only special people receive this gift, but instead, all Christians can receive the gift of specific healing for a specific disease. The believer receives the full authority of Christ through the Holy Spirit, and as a result, all diseases are subject to healing

## CONCLUSION:

There should be a great expectation in the church that every kind of disease, from physical to mental to spiritual, can be healed by the power of the Holy Spirit. It is clearly God's plan to empower believers in the Lord Jesus Christ to receive the gifts of healing. In the Scripture review, we have seen the healing ministry progress from an exclusive work of God the Father to God the Son, from God the Son to the apostles, and from the Holy Spirit to every Christian baptized in the Holy Spirit. As modern-day Christians, we should confidently activate the gift of healing so that those we lay hands on may be healed regardless of their condition.

**Notes:**

# *Sixteen*

# THE BEHAVIOR OF LOVE

**T**ext: *⁴ Love is patient and kind. Love is not jealous, it does not brag, and it is not proud. ⁵ Love is not rude, is not selfish, and does not get upset with others. Love does not count up wrongs that have been done. ⁶ Love is not happy with evil but is happy with the truth. ⁷ Love patiently accepts all things. It always trusts, always hopes, and always remains strong.* **1 Corinthians 13:4-7 (NCV)**

*²² But the Spirit produces the fruit of love, joy, peace, patience, kindness, goodness, faithfulness, ²³ gentlenesses, self-control.* **Galatians 5:22-23 (NCV)**

## INTRODUCTION:

According to Scripture, our lives need to be filled with love. (Ephesians 5:1-2) To show our love for Jesus, we have to keep his commandments. (John 15:9-11) However, his commandments dictate that we, first of all, love God and then we love each other. (Matthew 22:38) It is vital then that we stay in love and that we show that love not only to God but to each other through specific acts or behaviors which fulfill the commandments of Christ. What is this love and how do we show it?

## THE LOVE AND THE FRUIT:

In our text today, Paul outlines several behaviors which he defines as love. It's interesting to note that many of these behaviors are mentioned as the fruit of the Holy Spirit. Love itself is mentioned, of course, but so is patience, kindness, and self-control.

- We cannot mature in Christian love without walking in the Spirit.
- While the fruit of the Spirit is not earned, it can be practiced and developed.
- What we lack in ourselves due to our character defects will be provided for by the Holy Spirit. In other words, it is not possible to live a life of love without living a life filled with the Spirit.
- Please note that the fruit of the Spirit often develops during periods of conflict as well as offense.
- Because of this need to experience testing and trials, love will emerge to give us victory.
- God loves us in the same way that he asks us to love others. That is to say; he is patient and kind to us.

## THE DIMENSIONS OF LOVE:

The positive dimension: (what it is)

1. Is patient: The key to being able to love people is to see them not just as they are but as they will be if they walk in the Spirit and fully trust the Lord. Being patient with others enables acceptance and tolerance of their faults today for the sake of their growth tomorrow.

2. Is kind: A kind response is a response without aggression. Aggression can be physical, verbal, or social but kindness cancels the attack. To be kind means we choose the least aggressive response in any given situation.

3. Is happy with the truth: People attempt to hide from or escape from the truth. It takes the realization that the truth is the best possible outcome to appreciate it and be happy when it occurs in a relationship

4. Accepts all things: To accept all things does not mean that we want or desire all things to happen. The key to accepting all things is to understand that every aspect of one's life is in the hands of God. He is not taken by surprise when unfortunate things happen in our lives. We can feel safe and secure even in the worst circumstance when we believe that God is in control of the situation.

5. Always trusts: Ultimately, the one we must trust in is God. Because we want to control our own lives we often do not

trust God for the best possible outcome in any given situation. Scripture tells us that with all our heart we must trust the Lord and not our judgment or understanding. A measure of our spiritual maturity is the growth of love for God as a transition in which we trust ourselves less and him much more

6. Always hopes: A life of depression and despair is a life without hope. Once again, Christ is our hope. Because of him we always have the hope of victory in any given situation.

7. Always remains strong: For love to grow stronger, we must make it a practice of living a life of love. The more we love, the more we will be able to love.

The negative dimension: (what it is not)

- Not jealous: The basis of jealousy is fear combined with envy. We fear that we will lose or that somebody will gain more than what we have. Jealousy then motivates us to try to possess what other people have. Love rejoices in the blessings received by other people.

- Not prone to boasting: Boasting is primarily a method by which we praise ourselves. To use a colloquium, it is, "singing your own praises." The problem with boasting is that it leaves no room for anyone else and therefore prevents sharing of love.

- Not proud: The basis for being proud is usually feeling inadequate as a person in some manner. The person who is proud prevents sharing of love because it takes two to love and only one to be filled with pride.

- Not rude: Rudeness is a form of aggression and as such is an expression of unloving feelings rather than loving feelings. Impoliteness includes what you do as well as what you say.

- Not selfish: The Christian form of love demands self-sacrifice, and selfishness is the opposite of Christian love. Selfishness is the last retreat for those who cannot either give or receive love.

- Not easily offended: All offense produces anger, and anger prevents love from being expressed. A person who is easily offended mainly experiences constant outrage instead of comprehensive love.

- Not holding an offense: Holding offenses sometimes is called holding a grudge. Holding a grudge implies a lack of the ability to forgive.
- Not happy with evil: To be happy when evil falls upon a person implies a lack of love. Such a person very often is filled with hatred, anger, resentment, bitterness, and is driven by the memory of old offenses and hurts.

## CONCLUSION:

To practice love there are certain things that we must do, and things that we must avoid doing. If we are to live a life of love, we must exercise our will and practice loving others and loving God. If we practice those things that do not lead to love, we should not be astonished at the fact that our life is not filled with love but with the opposite of love. In all cases, we must realize that we need the help of the Holy Spirit and the fruit that the Holy Spirit gives us to love others as Christ loved us truly.

## NOTES:

# *Seventeen*

# THE MYSTERY OF
# DOUBTING THOMAS

T**ext:** *25 The other followers kept telling Thomas, "We saw the Lord." But Thomas said, "I will not believe it until I see the nail marks in his hands and put my finger where the nails were and put my hand into his side." (**John 20:25(NCV)**)*

*24Thomas (called Didymus), who was one of the twelve, was not with them when Jesus came. 25 The other followers kept telling Thomas, "We saw the Lord." But Thomas said, "I will not believe it until I see the nail marks in his hands and put my finger where the nails were and put my hand into his side." 26A week later the followers were in the house again, and Thomas was with them. The doors were locked, but Jesus came in and stood right in the middle of them. He said, "Peace be with you." 27 Then he said to Thomas, "Put your finger here, and look at my hands. Put your hand here in my side. Stop being an unbeliever and believe." 28Thomas said to him, "My Lord and my God!"*

*29 Then Jesus told him, "You believe because you see me. Those who believe without seeing me will be truly happy." **John 20:24-29 (NCV)***

## INTRODUCTION:

There is indeed a mystery in Thomas's reaction to the news of the resurrection of Jesus from the dead. Thomas was doubtful and declared that he would not believe until he had evidence that he could touch and feel. In other words, Thomas insisted that Jesus prove his resurrection. The question is why did Thomas take this position? What were possible factors involved in his insistence on evidence and not faith? There are at least three possible reasons that explain his behavior.

## 1. LOYALTY TO JESUS:

- Thomas was loyal to Jesus unto the death. In fact, it was Thomas who suggested that the apostles stay with Jesus even if they die in the process. (John 11:16).
- Because he was so loyal to Jesus, he needed proof that it was really Jesus who came back from the dead.
- The proof he needed would identify Jesus as the same person who was crucified. The evidence was the marks of the crucifixion.

## 2. A NEED FOR ORDER:

Thomas may have been one of those people that need to have a world which is in order and which does not deviate from what is the expected routine outcome.

- If this is the case, then Thomas would have a hard time believing in the resurrection because all his worldly experience tells him that those who are dead stay dead.
- To accept the fact of the resurrection without evidence, would ask Thomas to acknowledge that sometimes ordinary reality can be different than what he expects.
- Fundamentally, the resurrection of Jesus would shake up the world of Thomas and illustrate that with God even resurrection is possible.
- This would be very difficult for Thomas to accept just on faith and so he demanded physical evidence that a physical miracle took place.
- Thomas was resisting change to what he believed was possible, and normal.

## 3. A LOW LEVEL OF FAITH:

Belief in the resurrection demands a high level of faith because Jesus had not only returned from the dead, but he was resurrected in a new body that was immortal, indestructible, and highly empowered.

- This Scripture would indicate that Thomas was making a choice to be an unbeliever. What this means is that he did not have sufficient faith in the resurrection to overcome his unbelief in the resurrection.

- Notice that Jesus did not reject Thomas! Instead, Jesus provided Thomas with the physical evidence that he needed to believe.
- Once that physical evidence was provided, then Thomas was commanded to believe.
- At that point, Thomas could believe because he had the evidence that he demanded, and once that evidence was presented Thomas reacted by acknowledging the Godhood of Jesus.
- In other words, the transformation which took place in Thomas was about Thomas recognizing the divinity of Christ, because the resurrection demands a divine intervention.
- Thomas then recognized that Christ is God and declared him to be his God by calling him his Lord and God.

## CONCLUSION:

There's a little bit of Thomas in each of us. Our faith is not uniform; there are areas in which we have a firm belief and areas in which we have weak belief. Jesus would encourage us to strengthen the areas in which we are strong, but also to correct the areas of faith in which we are weak. Doubt is not a sin but is a detriment to fullness in our life in Christ. Jesus is happy and delighted to work with us to increase our faith. He also told us that faith brings happiness to our lives. The primary reward of faith, then, is our ability to maintain our peace, contentment, confidence, and joy in the Lord.

## NOTES:

## *Eighteen*

# RECEIVE THE BREATH OF THE HOLY SPIRIT

**T**ext: *¹When the day of Pentecost came, they were all together in one place. ²Suddenly a noise like a strong, blowing wind came from heaven and filled the whole house where they were sitting. ³They saw something like flames of fire that were separated and stood over each person there. ⁴They were all filled with the Holy Spirit, and they began to speak different languages by the power the Holy Spirit was giving them.* **Acts 2:1-4 (NCV)**

*²¹Then Jesus said again, "Peace be with you. As the Father sent me, I now send you." ²²After he said this, he breathed on them and said, "Receive the Holy Spirit. ²³If you forgive anyone his sins, they are forgiven. If you don't forgive them, they are not forgiven." **John 20:21-23 (NCV)***

## INTRODUCTION:

Throughout the Bible, the Holy Spirit is referred to as the breath of God, as in Genesis 1. The Hebrew word for spirit is "Rûach" which means a strong or even violent exhalation. The implication of both these Scriptures is that we all should receive the breath of God. However, most Christians do not know this or misunderstand what it means. So, the question remains: Why should I be baptized with the Holy Spirit? Why should I breathe in the breath of God?

## THE PROBLEM:

Like the disciples in John 20, every believer in Jesus Christ receives the Holy Spirit at conversion.

- Some teach, incorrectly, that this initial experience with the breath of God is the same experience described in Acts 2, which is the Baptism of the Holy Spirit.
- This erroneous teaching leads some to believe that they already have the Baptism of the Holy Spirit because they automatically receive the Spirit when they were saved.
- Ultimately, this rejection of the Baptism of the Holy Spirit means that we have many "breathless" Christians.

## THE FOUR BENEFITS:

To receive the full benefits of a relationship with the Holy Spirit, you need the Baptism of the Holy Spirit for the following reasons:

1. The Baptism of the Holy Spirit allows dynamic interaction with the person of the Holy Spirit.
2. The Baptism of the Holy Spirit focuses your spiritual sensibilities on Christ and the kingdom of God rather than Satan and his worldly works.
3. The Baptism of the Holy Spirit empowers the Christian for service through the spiritual gifts mentioned in 1 Corinthians 12.
4. The Baptism of the Holy Spirit, which results in personal and daily interaction with the Spirit, allows us to walk a better walk because we have his guidance and wisdom to sustain us during bad times.

## THE OUT OF BREATH CHRISTIAN

If you have not received Christ, then you have not taken your first spiritual breath because you are spiritually dead. Come alive and breathe in the Savior, and you will take your first deep breath.

- If you are a Christian, who has not received the Baptism in the Holy Spirit, you are breathing, but each breath is labored and difficult. You soon need more breath to walk your walk in Christ.
- Breathless Christians are not empowered to receive the gifts of the Spirit so they cannot overcome obstacles placed in their path by the Devil. They are defeated.
- Breathless Christians tend to substitute religion for a relationship.
- Breathless Christians often feel helpless and hopeless because they cannot draw upon the power of God.

- Breathless Christians get tired quickly, so they do not serve the Lord.
- Breathless Christians need outside support just to breathe, so they often become legalistic and judgmental.

## CONCLUSION

If you have not received the Baptism of the Holy Spirit and would like to receive, then ask for it so we can pray for you. We will also instruct you on what happens and what evidence you will experience to prove that you have been baptized in the Holy Spirit.

## NOTES:

# *Nineteen*

# CHRIST AND THE HOLY SPIRIT

**T**ext: *¹⁸"The Lord has put his Spirit in me, because he appointed me to tell the Good News to the poor. He has sent me to tell the captives they are free and to tell the blind that they can see again.* (Isaiah 61:1) *God sent me to free those who have been treated unfairly* (Isaiah 58:6) **Luke 4:18 (NCV)**

## INTRODUCTION:

What role should the Holy Spirit have in your Christian life? If we look at the relationship between Jesus and the Holy Spirit, we can answer that question and then move forward in union with the Holy Spirit of God.

## JESUS AND SPIRIT:

The Scriptures indicate that Jesus related to the Spirit in several essential ways to fulfill his mission on earth. Here are a few ways that Jesus and the Spirit interacted:

- Jesus was filled with the Spirit. *¹Jesus, filled with the Holy Spirit, returned from the Jordan River. The Spirit led Jesus into the desert* **Luke 4:1 (NCV)** Jesus being filled with the Spirit was not a one-time event. Every aspect of his mission and sense of unity with God the Father was facilitated by the fact that he was Spirit-filled. The same should be said of all Christians, because when we first believe we receive the presence of the Spirit. Our consciousness of the Spirit should be a daily blessing.

- Jesus was anointed by the Spirit. *³⁸You know about Jesus from Nazareth, that God gave him the Holy Spirit and power. You know how Jesus went everywhere doing good and healing those who were ruled by the devil because God was with him.* **Acts 10:38 (NCV)**

Jesus received power from the Holy Spirit to declare the kingdom of God. As Jesus used this power, he offered proof that he was the long-awaited Messiah.

- Christians of today can also obtain an anointing of the Holy Spirit to be empowered. The anointing happens to all baptized with the Holy Spirit.
- Jesus had the joy of the Holy Spirit. *²¹Then Jesus rejoiced in the Holy Spirit.* **Luke 10:21 (NCV)** Jesus experienced true rejoicing because God had given wonderful gifts to those who were like children and who could now operate with the power to overcome the Devil's works. The anointing still gives joy to those who do the will of Father God by serving the common good.

## THE BLIND:

Of all the miracles that Jesus performed, giving sight to the blind was one of his most numerous healings. Restoring vision is a significant miracle for several reasons:

- No one had restored vision to a blind person in the Old Testament, and there is no recorded case where a disciple of Christ restored the sight of a blind person. Jesus doing so was a declaration that he is the Messiah.
- In the Old Testament, giving sight to the blind was the sole right of God. (Exodus 4:11) Since Jesus gave sight to numerous blind people, he was declaring that he is God and one with Father God.
- All the healings of the blind people were done through the power of the Holy Spirit. Indeed, the Holy Spirit was helping Jesus declare his messiahship by working miracles.
- The people were healed under different conditions, situations, and numbers. Some were group healings (Matthew 9: 27-41), general population healings (Matthew 15:30), and individual healings (John 9). All these were done because the Holy Spirit was available to Jesus regardless of circumstances, once again showing us that the Spirit of God is not limited to just church settings.

Jerome A. Jochem M.S., M.A.

## WHAT ABOUT US?

Jesus is God, and so he not only had the power and the support of the Holy Spirit but could work miracles by his own power. We do not qualify in that manner, so we are dependent on the Holy Spirit to do the spiritual work needed as a testimony to Christ. To do this, we need to keep specific facts in mind:

- Receiving the Spirit is not the same as being empowered by the Spirit. The apostles of Jesus received the Spirit before they were empowered by the Spirit. For example, the apostles received the Spirit when Jesus breathed on them before Pentecost, but they were empowered by the Spirit at Pentecost. (John 20:21, Acts 2:1-13)

- When Jesus breathed on the apostles, he authorized them to forgive sins and to preach the good news, but when the apostles received the Spirit at Pentecost, they were enabled to work miracles as signs about the truth of Jesus.

- Just as there is no other way to salvation except through Christ, there is no other way of working Godly miracles except through the anointing of the Holy Spirit. Anything done outside of the influence or presence of the Spirit is demonic and should be avoided at all costs.

## CONCLUSION:

Jesus is our model. He showed us how we need to relate to the Holy Spirit and submit to him to work miracles to prove that Jesus is the only Messiah. Christianity is one of the most supernatural religions in the world, so Christians should not be shy about demonstrating the power of the Holy Spirit and establishing once and for all that Jesus is Lord of all.

## NOTES:

# THE HOLY SPIRIT AS A FIRE

**T**ext: *³They saw something like flames of fire that were separated and stood over each person there. ⁴They were all filled with the Holy Spirit, and they began to speak different languages by the power the Holy Spirit was giving them."* **Acts 2:3-4 (NCV)**

*⁴The Lord will wash away the filth from the women of Jerusalem. He will wash the bloodstains out of Jerusalem and clean the city with the spirit of fairness and the spirit of fire. "* **Isaiah 4:4 (NCV)**

## INTRODUCTION

Because the Holy Spirit is a rather mysterious person and somewhat difficult to understand, he is described by using symbols. Today we will discuss the symbol of fire. The Holy Spirit appeared like flames in the Book of Acts. In the Book of Hebrews, Scripture describes God as a consuming fire, and Isaiah spoke of God as a spirit of fire. What fire means to each person depends on their past experiences with fire. Some remember Christmas Eve around the fireplace with family and have warm feelings of love and enjoyment. Some remember being burned and the pain and loss that fire caused.

## WHEN GOD USES FIRE:

When God uses fire to represent the Holy Spirit, it is always for a positive reason and to accomplish beneficial purposes. Throughout Scripture, God showed us the fire of his Holy Spirit through:

- The burning bush of Moses.
- The brazen altar of the tabernacle.
- The fire of Mount Carmel.

- The 120 in the upper room who received Holy Spirit fire.

## GOD'S FIRE TODAY:

God's fire is not in some exterior place like the brazen altar but is in the hearts of his people.

- All Christians have the Holy Spirit within them, so they have the potential of releasing his fire.
- The sad fact is that not all have released that potential. Maybe the majority has rejected it.
- To release the fire, a Christian must be empowered through the Baptism of the Holy Spirit.

## AS A SYMBOL OF FIRE:

The Holy Spirit does what fire does. Fire burns things up and cleans us up.

*³But today remember that the LORD your God goes in before you to destroy them like a fire that burns things up. He will defeat them ahead of you, and you will force them out and destroy them quickly, just as the LORD has said.* **Deuteronomy 9:3 (NCV)**

- In Ephesus, they burned the books of magic under the command of the Holy Spirit (Acts 19:19)
- The sin of Sodom caused the fire which destroyed the entire city.
- When the people exposed Achan's sin, they stoned him and burned him with fire (Josh. 7:25).

The fire of the Holy Spirit will burn away or consume all the undesirable and ungodly character traits in us and replace them with the wonderful fruit of the Holy Spirit. *²²But the Spirit produces the fruit of love, joy, peace, patience, kindness, goodness, faithfulness, ²³gentleness, self-control.* **Galatians 5:22 (NCV)**

So, the fire burns up the opposite of the fruit - hate, depression, fear/anxiety, impatience, meanness, evil, disloyalty, harshness, and self-indulgence.

## FIRE PREPARES:

*⁹When the followers stepped out of the boat and onto the shore, they saw a fire of hot coals. There were fish on the fire, and there was bread.* **John 21:9 (NCV)**

Many times, when we are walking through a fire in our lives, it is the hand of God preparing us for what he wants of us.

- We may refuse to allow the fire in our lives and rebel against the Holy Spirit because we neither trust him nor believe he is in control.
- We need to allow God to bring forth his fire so that we are ready to serve him.

## FIRE BRINGS HOPE:

To those lost in darkness, a burning lamp brings the hope of rescue and salvation.

- The flame of the Holy Spirit in you is the hope that the world needs to see.
- Are you hiding that hope under a basket? When the world looks at you what does it see? Does it recognize the flame burning within you?
- We all must burn brightly as the darkness grows in our nation and the world.
- We are not raptured out of this world yet, and so we must burn brightly to avoid fatalism.

## FIRE TRANSFORMS:

*2 As wax melts before a fire, let the wicked be destroyed before God.* **Psalms 68:2 (NCV)**

*2 Like a fire that burns twigs, like a fire that makes water boil, let your enemies know who you are. Then all nations will shake with fear when they see you.* **Isaiah 64:2 (NCV)**

Don't kid yourself, there are some genuine enemies of Christianity and of the church who are very active in our country today, and they are on the attack against people of faith and the standards of morality which we hold dear.

- This is happening because we are not burning bright. No one is opposing these ungodly decisions and countering the attempt to dehumanize Christians as "religious bigots."

- The fire of the Holy Spirit will touch the hearts of these people and soften them. This is the only way that they can be regenerated and have a real transformation of spirit and mind.
- What can you do? Pray and pray hard that a nationwide revival takes place - that the fire of the Holy Spirit pushes back the darkness and hate which are overtaking our nation.
- For the church to burn bright, it must be united by the fire. Our divisions and conflicts have weakened us. We must reach unity because fellowship is dependent on the flame.

## 5. FIRE ENABLES POWER:
*⁸But when the Holy Spirit comes to you, you will receive power....”* **Acts 1:8 (NCV)**

You can both receive and give out the power within you.
- No Christian is genuinely flameless.
- If your flame is low, then asked for a rekindling - a renewing of the fire.
- If you are glowing bright, they share the light.

## CONCLUSION:
Let us set our souls afire! Let us share the flame of the Holy Spirit. Let us shine brightly in the ever-growing darkness.

## NOTES:

# Twenty - One

# THE SEAL - A SYMBOL OF THE HOLY SPIRIT

**T**ext: *"Do not grieve the Holy Spirit of God, with whom you were sealed for the day of redemption"* **Ephesians. 4:30 (NIV)**.

## INTRODUCTION

In a recent conversation with a friend, I said that I have not even touched the depth of the content found in God's Word. The Bible is so deeply layered with information and wisdom that it is nearly impossible to understand it all. As an example, we find this layering in Ephesians. 4:30 because it contains three independent concepts, a theological doctrine, and a symbol of the Holy Spirit:

- Concept 1 is that we should not grieve the Holy Spirit of God.
- Concept 2 is that we were sealed in the Holy Spirit.
- Concept 3 is that the sealing by the Holy Spirit is for the day of redemption.
- The theological doctrine is that of our redemption. The symbol of the Holy Spirit is that of a seal.

## GRIEVING THE HOLY SPIRIT:

The Holy Spirit is a person, so he has emotions.

- Most human communication is 80% emotional and only 20% intellectual.
- Faith to be complete must also be 80/20% - no such thing as being too emotional.

- We are made in the image of God so God must also be an 80/20% person.
- Jesus had a full set of emotions, including grief.
- Grief, as used in this Scripture, means to bring sorrow.
- Grief results from many things, including an offense and the loss of a loved one.
- Grief is one of the most influential human emotions and if excessive can bring death.
- Paul warned us not to grieve like unbelievers without hope. (1 Thessalonians 4:13)
- It is incredible to me that the Spirit of God is grieved by our actions: (Vs. 31)
    o Bitterness.
    o Anger.
    o Wrath.
    o Quarreling.
    o Evil behavior.
    o Slanderous talk.

Why do these things grieve the Holy Spirit? The Holy Spirit is grieved because these emotions and attitudes separate him from us. Our personal relationship with him is broken, and that grieves him. These things can restore our covenant with him:

- Knowing that he can be grieved, we should keep in mind that he is watching and listening.
- We need to develop the determination not to grieve him by what we do and what we say.
- If we have grieved him, we must be sensitive to the need to ask forgiveness and then repent.
- When we grieve him, we are quenching his power within us.

## THE SEAL:
This Scripture tells us that the Holy Spirit acts as a seal.

A seal is used in the Bible to:

- Establish privacy for documents. (Like to seal a letter)
- Prohibit entrance to chambers (Like the tomb of Jesus)
- Confirm instructions in letters.

- Ratify covenants. Which I think is the meaning of the seal in Ephesians 4:30.

## WHAT DOES THE SEAL DO?

The love of the Holy Spirit gives birth to the new creation which is sealed with the signature of Christ.

God knows that we are part of the New Covenant written in the Blood of Christ because we are imprinted body, mind, and spirit with the character of Jesus Christ developed in time by the Holy Spirit. God the Father knows we belong to him because of the Seal.

It is very important to know that the Devil does not have the authority or power to break this seal off us. *¹Then I saw a scroll in the right hand of the One sitting on the throne. The scroll had writing on both sides and was kept closed with seven seals. ²And I saw a powerful angel calling in a loud voice, "Who is worthy to break the seals and open the scroll?" ³But there was no one in heaven or on earth or under the earth who could open the scroll or look inside it. ⁴I cried hard because there was no one who was worthy to open the scroll or look inside. ⁵But one of the elders said to me, "Do not cry! The Lion from the tribe of Judah, David's descendant, has won the victory so that he is able to open the scroll and its seven seals."*
**Revelation 5:1-5 (NCV)**

- No angel, man, or the Devil could break the seven seals.
- No angel, no man, nor devil and remove the seal of the Holy Spirit from you.
- Still, we have this warning. We can grieve the Holy Spirit by breaking the seal ourselves. Not because we occasionally sin and then repent, but only if we adopt sin as a lifestyle. We can remove the seal ourselves, and the Holy Spirit will stay grieved until we return to Christ.

## THE DAY OF REDEMPTION:

Redemption is a theological term which is part of the language of our salvation.

- It means to purchase back something that is lost.
- Also, it has the meaning of obtaining something which belongs to someone else for a price.

Jerome A. Jochem M.S., M.A.

An early example of Biblical redemption is in the Book of Numbers:

*[11]The LORD also said to Moses, [12]"I am choosing the Levites from all the Israelites to take the place of all the firstborn children of Israel. The Levites will be mine, [13]because the firstborn are mine. When you were in Egypt, I killed all the firstborn children of the Egyptians and took all the firstborn of Israel to be mine, both animals, and children. They are mine. I am the LORD."* **Numbers 3:11-13 (NCV)**

Jesus paid the price to redeem us from the possession of the Devil. He is our Redeemer, and we belong to him at our salvation.

If we are already redeemed by Jesus, what did Paul mean that we are sealed "for the day of Redemption? All the terms used to describe our salvation experience have three tenses. For example, we can say:

- Salvation – I have been saved, I am being saved, I will be saved.
- Justification – I have been justified, I am being justified, I will be justified.
- Sanctified – I have been sanctified, I am being sanctified, I will be sanctified.

Also, for redemption:

- I have been redeemed by the blood of Christ.
- I am being redeemed by the mercy of Christ.
- I will be redeemed by the resurrection of Christ.

Paul was referring to that day when we are resurrected and fully and finally redeemed from this world and sin.

## CONCLUSIONS:

We should always keep in mind the simple fact that the Bible is profound and allow ourselves to drink deeply of its wisdom and guidance. The Holy Spirit is a person in relationship with us. If we love him, then we will take care not to offend him. The Holy Spirit seals us, and we bear the signature of Christ. We should live like it. We are still a work in progress. That fact demands patience and endurance with ourselves and other Christians.

NOTES:

# Twenty-Two

# THE GIVER OF GIFTS

**T**ext: *¹⁷Every good action and every perfect gift is from God. These good gifts come down from the Creator of the sun, moon, and stars, who does not change like their shifting shadows.* **James 1:17 (NCV)**

## INTRODUCTION:

As our culture becomes more secular, the focus of Christmas and other such holidays is concerned with the giving of gifts rather than receiving Christ.

- The saddest part of this trend is that Santa Claus and the Easter Bunny have become the giver of gifts rather than God.
- And yet, God in his mercy does give humanity gifts, and these gifts represent his love, especially for those who are his children.
- God has demonstrated this gift-giving love in both the Old and the New Testaments.

## THE GIFTS OF THE OLD TESTAMENT:

The Gift of Life:

The Book of Genesis tells us that God made a human form from the earth, and then breathed life into that form. Thus, God created Adam and from Adam God created Eve.

- The first gift God gave was that of life.
- Life is very mysterious. Although modern-day science would try to convince us that life originated from dead things that idea is highly unlikely.

- Using nonliving chemicals, no one has created life in the test tube or the lab. The closest science has come to create a variation of a cell was by using living parts of already existing cells. And so, to Adam and Eve, it was God who gave the precious gift of life.

The Gift of Covenant:

Adam and Eve had children, some of which, like Enoch, had a special relationship with God. However, to find the next great gift that God gave you need to look at Abraham.

- The gift that God gave Abraham was one of a covenant.
- Through his covenant relationship with Abraham, God agreed to prosper Abraham throughout his life and to prosper Abraham's children for many generations.
- Abraham had children, and his children had children, one of whom was a man called Jacob. God changed Jacob's name to Israel. Because of God's covenant with Abraham, a nation was founded, a country which still exists today.
- The most significant gift that God gave Abraham was his covenant agreement that laid the foundation for the establishment of an entire nation.

The Gifts of Power and Freedom:

- Jacob, now Israel, had sons, one of whom was Joseph, who led Israel into Egypt. Israel ended up in bondage and slavery in Egypt for 400 years.
- God, then choose a man called Moses to give a gift of supernatural power of such great strength that it freed Israel from the grip of Egyptian bondage. Israel was set free by the gift of God.
- In this case, Moses was a gift designated from his birth by God to bless and free Israel, and Moses received the gift of supernatural power to achieve that end.

The Gift of Praise and Worship:

Now we must leap ahead in the history of Israel through the judges and until the time of the kings. We'll focus on one king; whose name was David.

- David was a great warrior, a great soldier, a great sinner, and a great poet. That latter gift established what we now call "Davidic" worship.
- Davidic worship is passionate adoration, active praise, and God derived contact with the Holy Spirit.

The Gifts of Prophetic Men:

Throughout the Old Testament, you will find God giving Israel gifts of men who prophesied. Some of these prophetic men are known as major prophets, and some are known as minor prophets.

- As Israel stumbled through the world on its way to its final destiny, God gave men who spoke prophesy as a means of guidance and as a warning of coming punishment.
- Very often the leadership of Israel did not respond well to these prophetic men, but that didn't stop God in his mercy from giving them in the hope that Israel would repent and change its ways.

## GIFTS OF THE NEW TESTAMENT:

There is a parallel between the gifts of the Old Testament and the gifts in the New Testament. Perhaps the only significant difference is that the giving of the gifts in the New Testament is greatly accelerated. Through Christ, mankind received the bounty of God, with greater intensity and frequency than ever before.

The Gift of Life:

In the New Testament, there are two dimensions to the gift of life.

- The first dimension is the life given to Christ in the incarnation. This is a reflection of the life given to Adam and Eve in Genesis. Although Christ's body is not formed out of the earth, but through the natural process of birth, that body still needed the miracle of life, and God gave that miracle through the Holy Spirit so that Christ might be born.
- The second dimension is an eternal life given by Christ to all those who believe in him. It is God's breath that has no end, in as much as we draw upon the very life of God to maintain our own life.

The Gift of Covenant:
Abraham received the first covenant. Jesus won the last covenant.

*²⁷Then he took the cup, gave thanks and offered it to them, saying, "Drink from it, all of you. ²⁸This is my blood of the covenant, which is poured out for many for the forgiveness of sins.* **Matthew 26:27-28 (NIV)**

- Unlike the first covenant, the last covenant prospers not just the nation of Israel, but all those who believe in the Lord Jesus Christ.
- The last covenant is unlimited in its ability to establish a new nation made of anyone and everyone who believes in and accepts the work of Christ.
- The first covenant was sealed by the act of circumcision, while the last covenant is sealed by the sacrificial act of Christ, giving his body and his blood to establish a permanent relationship between God and believers for all eternity.
- The first covenant led to the law as a means of keeping it, while the last covenant is dependent upon grace as a means of implementing it.

The Gifts of Power and Freedom:
*⁸But when the Holy Spirit comes to you, you will receive power. You will be my witnesses—in Jerusalem, in all of Judea, in Samaria, and in every part of the world."* **Acts 1: 8 (NCV)**.

*⁷In Christ we are set free by the blood of his death, and so we have forgiveness of sins.* **Ephesians 1:7 (NCV)**.

Through Christ, the gifts of power and freedom are much more dynamic and comprehensive, then the gifts given to Moses.

- Notice that the Scripture in Acts tells us that we will receive power to physically change the world so that we might witness concerning Christ. Moses also received power to change the world through the ten miracles inflicted upon Egypt to convince Egypt to release Israel.
- The power that we receive, since it comes from the Holy Spirit, is not limited to a specific period or place.

- The freedom that we receive from Christ is spiritual because it releases us from bondage to the sinful nature. Israel was set free from slavery to the government of Egypt, but Christ's freedom liberates us from bondage to the government of Satan.

The Gift of Praise and Worship:

*23 The time is coming when the true worshipers will worship the Father in spirit and truth, and that time is here already. You see, the Father too is actively seeking such people to worship him.* **John 4:23 (NCV)**

- Davidic worship was primarily concerned with form.
- The gift of worship given to us by God through Christ has its focus on a relationship with God.
- Christ also revealed to us that God is seeking those who will worship him in spirit and truth.
- This gives a new and very supernatural aspect to worship, which transcends form and style.

The Gifts of Prophetic Men:

- In the Old Testament, God appointed a very few men out of the nation of Israel to gift them with prophecy.
- The New Testament communication gifts are much more comprehensive; they are part of the nine supernatural gifts mentioned in 1 Corinthians Chapter 12.
- These gifts are available to all Christians, not just a few selected people who would speak for God.
- In the Old Testament, God would give Israel the gifts of prophets, priests, and kings. Because Christ served in each one of these offices, he can provide the same roles in the church. (Ephesians 4:11-14)

## CONCLUSION:

The most significant gift is Christ because all the gifts flow through him. Christ is the ultimate expression of God's love for us and of his desire for us to love him. Let us not forget who is the great giver of gifts.

NOTES:

# Twenty-Three

# SACRED COWS AND MISSING PEARLS

INTRODUCTION:

Our faith in the Lord Jesus Christ is the most cherished possession that we can have in this world. Because our faith is precious, we need to keep it pure by making sure it is consistent with the Bible. Nevertheless, we all tend to fall into two errors of faith. The first error is beliefs that are "sacred cows," while the second error I call "missing pearls."

## SACRED COWS

- In India, the cow is venerated and even worshiped. In many of the individual states in India, it is illegal to kill a cow and may be considered an act of blasphemy.
- Even Mahatma Gandhi elevated the cow to the point of worship,
- Gandhi said: "I worship it and I shall defend its worship against the whole world," and that, "The central fact of Hinduism is cow protection." He regarded her better than the earthly mother and called her "the mother to millions of Indian mankind."[1] The main point here is that the elevation of a cow to the status of being "sacred" is based on mistaken religious notions. A perversion of religion described by Paul: *25They traded the truth of God for a lie. They worshiped and served what had been created instead of the God who created those things, who should be praised forever. Amen.* **Romans 1:25 (NCV)**

---

[1] *Compilation of Gandhi's views on Cow Protection." Dahd.nic.in. 7 July 1927. Retrieved 13 November 2011)*

- For Christians, the phrase sacred cow has come to mean a belief which is not based nor supported by Scripture but is often thought to be Scriptural.

## A CHRISTIAN SACRED COW:

Here is a very popular Christian sacred cow: "God will not give you more trials than you can handle."

- This saying is a form of counseling given to people who are having something catastrophic happening in their lives. Usually multiple attacks of the demonic.
- It is an adage which is meant to comfort and give hope; it is thought to be Scriptural, and it is accepted as such without question.
- This belief is a cherished sacred cow because it has no Biblical support whatsoever and, based on experience, is just not true.
- The Scripture that most think support this particular sacred cow is *[13] The only temptation that has come to you is that which everyone has. But you can trust God, who will not permit you to be tempted more than you can stand. But when you are tempted, he will also give you a way to escape so that you will be able to stand it.* **1 Corinthians 10:13 (NCV)**
- This scripture talks about temptations and not trials.
- Temptations almost always deal with things that you can control, but trials are out of your control and often happen against your desire and will.
- 1 Corinthians 10:13 does not support our sacred cow - and in fact, trials can build up to the point of intense suffering beyond what you can bear.
- Paul described such an experience in 2 Corinthians: *[8]Brothers and sisters, we want you to know about the trouble we suffered in Asia. We had great burdens there that were beyond our own strength. We even gave up hope of living. [9]Truly, in our own hearts we believed we would die. But this happened so we would not trust in ourselves, but in God, who raises people from the dead.* **2 Corinthians 1:8-9 (NCV)**
- Will God give you more trials than you can handle? Absolutely! But why?

- Paul tells us that when the trials become so intense and challenging, we should not depend on our strength but trust God to bear our burdens. Peter agreed when he wrote: *⁶Be humble under God's mighty hand so he will lift you up when the right time comes. ⁷Give all your worries to him, because he cares about you.* **1 Peter 5:6-7 (NCV)**
- How much better than a sacred cow is the promise of God that he will take up your burdens and deliver you from the suffering of your trials. How amazing he is that he will bear your burdens for you if you trust him.

## MISSING PEARLS

Missing pearls speak of what is lacking in our faith. Sometimes a lack of true understanding and appreciation of Scripture can add to our religious misdirection and set us off on the wrong path of faith.

## CHRIST IN US - A MISSING PEARL

Many people have a missing pearl concerning this Scripture: *¹³We know that we live in God and he lives in us because he gave us his Spirit. ¹⁴We have seen and can testify that the Father sent his Son to be the Savior of the world. ¹⁵Whoever confesses that Jesus is the Son of God has God living inside, and that person lives in God. ¹⁶And so we know the love that God has for us, and we trust that love. God is love. Those who live in love live in God, and God lives in them.* **1 John 4:13-16 (NCV)**

The missing pearl is the fact that many Christians do not understand what it means to have God living in them. The idea of Christ in you means that:

- Your relationship with Christ/God is established by trusting in Christ, not by how often, or long you pray or worship.
- We do not have to search for God because he is already in us and we are in him.
- We do need to abide in Christ. We need to recognize that we are living with and in him, but we do not need to force our spiritual growth through our efforts - abiding will cause us to grow at God's pace.
- We do not need to fear death because eternal life is within us.

- We do have a connection to the power of God through the Holy Spirit, and we are authorized to use that power as God commands.
- We do not need more and more of Jesus, but we need more and more of what we already have of him. Remember that we have all of Christ, not just part of him.
- We do not have to struggle to find a spiritual partner. We already have one in Christ, so we are never abandoned, alone and desolate.

## CONCLUSION:

Sacred cows hide the truth and misdirect us so that we believe what is false and limited. Missing pearls cause us to take a path of faith that is often frustrating and deceptive. We owe it to ourselves to eliminate the sacred cows and find the missing pearls of our faith.

## NOTES:

# *Twenty-Four*

## THE ASCENSION - SIX FACTS

**T**ext: *⁵¹ While he was blessing them, he was separated from them and carried into heaven.* **Luke 24:51 (NCV)**

*⁵⁰ Jesus led his followers as far as Bethany, and he raised his hands and blessed them. ⁵¹ While he was blessing them, he was separated from them and carried into heaven. ⁵² They worshiped him and returned to Jerusalem very happy. ⁵³ They stayed in the Temple all the time, praising God.* **Luke 24:50-53 (NCV)**

### INTRODUCTION:

While Ascension Day is as important as Christmas and Easter, it indeed is not celebrated equally, and in fact, may be ignored. One of the reasons for this is that Ascension Day is more challenging to understand than either of the other holidays. For example, we can know that Christ was born via the Holy Spirit on Christmas, and we can understand his resurrection from the dead-on Easter, but what in the world does the Ascension mean? In this sermon, I want to give some crucial facts about Ascension Day that every Christian should know and keep in mind when discussing the importance of Christ entering heaven.

### FROM EARTHLY TO HEAVENLY MINISTRY:

Jesus lived as a normal human being for approximately 30 years. After three years of intense ministry, he was crucified, he paid the price for our sin, and when he resurrected, he demonstrated the fact that God accepted his sacrifice as a ransom for us.

- On the day of Ascension, however, he leaves behind his earthly ministry and its inherent limitations and begins his ministry in heaven.
- This is a critical transition because now he is in heaven and the Holy Spirit is in charge of his church.
- You might take note that he did not change into a spirit before this transition took place, but instead, he ascended bodily into heaven.
- Also note, that it was not his pre-resurrection body that ascended, but rather the body he had after his resurrection.

## THE RETURN TO HEAVENLY GLORY:

During his earthly ministry, Jesus set aside his glory. Those that saw him saw only a man and not the God-man.

- Only once during his earthly ministry did a few of his disciples see his true glory, and that was at the Transfiguration. (Matthew 17:1 – 9)
- Mostly, it was at the Ascension that Jesus returned to the glory that he originally had before the incarnation.
- There were several times that Jesus said that he was looking forward to returning to the glory that he had with the Father before he began his earthly ministry. The Ascension is a description of the return to his glory.
- Because Christ returns to his glory in heaven, we will also experience glory, which is a promise to believers. *⁴ Christ is our life, and when he comes again, you will share in his glory.* **Colossians 3:4 (NCV)**
- The glory of God through Christ will one day fill the earth. *¹⁴ For the earth will be filled with the knowledge of the glory of the LORD, as the waters cover the sea.* **Habakkuk 2:14 (NIV)**

## THE NEW HIGH PRIEST:

*¹⁴ Since we have a great high priest, Jesus the Son of God, who has gone into heaven, let us hold on to the faith we have. ¹⁵ For our high priest is able to understand our weaknesses. When he lived on earth, he was tempted in every way that we are, but he did not sin.* **Hebrews 4:14-15 (NCV)**

The Ascension established Christ as our new high priest. This means that he intercedes for us as we live our daily lives.

- Hebrews tells us that we have a high priest in heaven who understands the human condition, our human weaknesses, and character faults because he experienced them, but did not sin.
- The fact that our high priest lived among us as a human being but is now exalted to the right hand of God means that we have an advocate who will stand for us because he sympathizes with us.
- Because Christ is our high priest, and because he does understand our situation, we can expect an understanding and compassionate ear as we plead our case based on his sacrifice on the cross.

## THE STAMP OF SUCCESS:

The Ascension of Christ into heaven signified the fact that all he had set out to do during his earthly ministry was successful.

- His ascension was the final stamp of accomplishment.
- It is a supernatural recognition that he had achieved and completed all he had set out to do for us and was entirely successful in the work that his Father had given him.

## THE FATHER'S ACCEPTANCE:

[9] So *then after the Lord had spoken unto them, he was received up into heaven, and sat on the right hand of God.* **Mark 16:19 (KJV).** Notice the phrase in the King James Version, which says that he was "received up" into heaven. This would imply that God the Father agreed to his ascension and welcomed him back to heaven.

- The Ascension, then, represents the Father's exaltation of his son.
- When Christ ascended, he received all power and authority from his Father.
- Scripture says that the Father gave him this authority and power: [21] God *has put Christ over all rulers, authorities, powers, and kings, not only in this world but also in the next.* [22] *God put everything under his power and made him the head over everything for the church,* [23] *which is Christ's body. The church is filled with Christ, and Christ fills everything in every way.* **Ephesians 1:21-23 (NCV)**

## THE DAY OF HIS RETURN:

*[10] As he was going, they were looking into the sky. Suddenly, two men wearing white clothes stood beside them. [11] They said, "Men of Galilee, why are you standing here looking into the sky? Jesus, whom you saw taken up from you into heaven, will come back in the same way you saw him go. "* **Acts 1:10-11 (NCV)**

One of the most challenging aspects of the Ascension is the description of what the apostles saw as Jesus ascended into heaven.

- One gets the impression that he floated up into the sky and was eventually hidden by a cloud.
- We should understand that the description of the event given by the apostles was limited by their knowledge, perception, and understanding of the world. They had never seen such an event before. Therefore, it was difficult for them to describe it.
- In other words, the cloud, they saw may be like the spiritual cloud often referred to in the Old and New Testaments. It could have been like the glory cloud that filled the temple when Solomon dedicated it to the Lord, or the cloud they saw at the Transfiguration.
- Also, when he departed from them, it may mean that he left them in such a way that they needed to search for him by looking into the sky. He may not have floated up into the sky as so often depicted in the works of classical art.
- However, one thing is sure, that one day he will return as he ascended, and that return will have three characteristics:
    1. It will be a physical bodily return.
    2. He will return literally, that is, he will come back to the earth as a resurrected human who is also the Son of God.
    3. His return will be visible not only to a few, but the entire world, and his return will be in the clouds of glory, in which he left.

## CONCLUSION:

Jesus is in heaven, but he sent us the Holy Spirit, through whom we can reach out to him personally, and in prayer. He's there for us to guide us and counsel us and receive us when we too will journey to heaven. In the meantime, the Holy Spirit fulfills his orders and instructions for the church and us individually. Ascension Sunday is not the end, but the beginning of our eternal destiny.

NOTES:

# Twenty-Five

## THE DEVIL'S SCHEMES

**T**ext: *In order that Satan might not outwit us. For we are not unaware of his schemes.* **2 Corinthians 2:11 (NIV)**

### INTRODUCTION:

In this and other Scriptures, Satan is described as a spirit that can have a profound impact on our lives.

- As Christians, Satan will dramatically act against us individually and as a community.
- This Scripture implies that Satan attempts to plan out his attacks. He tries to nullify our defenses and find our weak areas to influence us.
- It is essential that we understand his plans and modes of attack so we can prevent them from defeating us individually and as a community.

### NATURE OF THE DEVIL:

The spirit we call the Devil was an angel (Lucifer or light bearer) who rebelled against God and convinced other angels to join him. He failed and then changed to a profane spirit who hates God and those who belong to God. Lucifer became Satan, and the angels that followed Satan became demons.

- The character and values of the Devil are reverse of God. The Devil became profane.
- Satan is not omnipresent or omnipotent. Satan cannot be in two places at once and has limited spiritual power. He can influence

only one person at a time. Very unlikely that any individual Christian has ever met Satan.

• The spirits that followed Satan (demons) represent him and carry out his orders and policies.

• While he is a person, he does not now nor never had a physical body. Since he is only a spirit, he must possess a body to have a material impact.

## AREAS OF ATTACK:

Satan is not an original and creative thinker. He is not inventing new temptations or tactics that make us fall away from God. In his schemes of attack, he operates in four primary areas and in only two modes. Remember that every attack is an attempt to weaken or destroy your faith in God.

1. Financial: The Devil will activate plans to ruin you economically by either reducing your income or swelling the amount you owe or both. These types of attacks are harder for him if you are tithing. Financial stress tends to weaken your faith in God as your provider and giver of blessings.

2. Relationships: The Devil will disrupt marriages and other relationships. He has a whole arsenal of weapons to use such as by planning sexual traps or by unresolved conflicts or by drug abuse. Relational stress weakens your faith in God's caring love by feeding resentment, bitterness, and anger towards God and church members.

3. Health: By stealing your good health, he attempts to paralyze and abort the plan of God in your life. Almost all his demons can produce some disease and they obey his general policy to spread as much illness as they can. Disease not only weakens your body but living in constant pain and sickness brings about depression, a feeling of hopelessness and helplessness.

4. Spirit: the minions of Satan will attack with doubt, confusion, and mental conflict (double-mindedness). Scripture warns us that Satan can cause severe problems in the church and Paul says: *But I am afraid that just as Eve was deceived by the serpent's cunning, your minds may somehow be led astray from your sincere and pure devotion to Christ.* **2 Corinthians 11:3 (NIV)**

## TWO MODES OF ATTACK:

*⁴⁴You belong to your father the devil, and you want to do what he wants. He was a murderer from the beginning and was against the truth, because there is no truth in him. When he tells a lie, he shows what he is really like, because he is a liar and the father of lies.* **John 8:44 (NCV)**

Just as Satan does not seem to be a creative thinker, he is equally limited as to how he approaches us. There are be two common modes of approach with the first mode being much more common than the second mode.

1. Persuasion: He tries seduction with a smile. He deceives with a welcome sign. He gives us a trusting lie. This is the way that Satan captivates Christians. Not by force, but by the soft voice of temptation. This is true to his nature as the "accuser." After all, he just persuaded the sinner to sin, the sinner made a choice to sin and therefore the sinner is guilty.

2. Aggression: *Be alert and of sober mind. ⁸Your enemy the devil prowls around like a roaring lion looking for someone to devour. ⁹Resist him, standing firm in the faith, because you know that the family of believers throughout the world is undergoing the same kind of sufferings.* **1 Peter 5:8-9 (NIV)**

The level of satanic aggression has varied over time and in different cultures. We need not strain to see the Devil's aggression all over the world as Christians are murdered and persecuted for their faith. His emotional attacks are most common especially fear, depression, and anger.

## HOW TO HAVE VICTORY:

*Put on the full armor of God, so that you can take your stand against the devil's schemes.* **Ephesians 6:11 (NIV)**

We are entirely able to stop Satan's attacks, but we must be armored in each area of attack.

- The helmet of salvation protects from the mental persuasion to sin.
- Sword of the Spirit protects against confusion and enables spiritual power.
- Shield of faith protects against temptations.

- Breastplate of righteousness protects against distortions of faith and practices.

## CONCLUSION:

We must resist the Devil and take the authority and power that Christ has given us to reject Satan's persuasion and deceptions from influencing us to sin. We must use the power and authority of Christ to rebuke Satan's aggression. *Jesus turned and said to Peter, "Get behind me, Satan! You are a stumbling block to me; you do not have in mind the concerns of God, but merely human concerns."* **Matthew 16:23 (NIV).**

## NOTES:

# WHEN I DIE

**ext:** *<sup>25</sup>Jesus said to her, "I am the resurrection and the life. Those who believe in me will have life even if they die. <sup>26</sup>And everyone who lives and believes in me will never die. Martha, do you believe this?"* **John 11:25 (NCV)**

*<sup>34</sup>Jesus said to them, "On earth, people marry and are given to someone to marry. <sup>35</sup>But those who will be worthy to be raised from the dead and live again will not marry, nor will they be given to someone to marry. <sup>36</sup>In that life they are like angels and cannot die. They are children of God, because they have been raised from the dead.* **Luke 20:34-36 (NCV)**

*<sup>51</sup>I tell you the truth, whoever obeys my teaching will never die."* **John 8:51 (NCV)**

*<sup>1</sup>Jesus said, "Don't let your hearts be troubled. Trust in God, and trust in me. <sup>2</sup>There are many rooms in my Father's house; I would not tell you this if it were not true. I am going there to prepare a place for you. <sup>3</sup>After I go and prepare a place for you; I will come back and take you to be with me so that you may be where I am.* **John 14:1-4 (NCV)**

## INTRODUCTION:

A universal question asked by most people is what will happen to me when I die? A second question is where I will go after I die? Since most everyone will die before the Lord returns these are appropriate questions to ask. There is an atmosphere of fear that surrounds death. We have all seen someone die and may have participated in the funeral. We don't like death, and we identify it as an enemy of life. In this sermon, I intend to explore what the Holy Scriptures tell us about death and the afterlife.

## NON-CHRISTIAN DOCTRINES:

Scientism/Materialism:

Two theories that have developed since the eighteenth century have become very popular:

1. Scientism is the elevation of science to a religion. Those who believe that scientific findings are inerrant and universally true tend to substitute scientific discoveries for spiritual doctrines. The problem is that the results of science are subject to change based on new information. Also, the foundation of scientism is materialism. Such a foundation limits observation and therefore, knowledge. In other words, science cannot prove or disprove the existence of God or an afterlife because materialism limits science. The religion of scientism allows no afterlife or God.

2. Materialism is the belief that the universe consists only of physical, measurable, and observable matter. To the materialist, death ends existence. Nothing survives once the brain is dead. There are no ghosts, spirits or a spiritual universe.

Both these theories are used to support a growing population of atheists.

Hebrew Sheol:

The Old Testament describes a "holding place" for departed spirits that is a shadowy and vague realm in which the spirit of a departed person is weak, less alive, non-physical, and less real than the living person. This essentially is a "ghost" of the once living person.

- Jesus believed that ghosts existed or at least he did not rebuke belief in ghosts when he told his apostles: *[39]Look at my hands and my feet. It is I myself! Touch me and see, because a ghost does not have a living body as you see I have."* **Luke 24:39 (NCV)**

- The existence of a Sheol like place seems to be confirmed by modern parapsychology. We must exercise caution when accepting out-of-body, after death, and "ghost hunting" data as proof that there is life after death, but the evidence seems overwhelming that the Old Testament Sheol still exists.

- This holding place is not the place of final judgment, contains only those who refused Christ during their lifetime, and like

Hades will end in the fiery lake. The Bible divides Sheol into two distinct places. The first place is called "Paradise" or the "Bosom of Abraham" and the second place is Hades or hell. (Luke 23:43, 2 Corinthians 12:3-4, Revelations 20:13)

Reincarnation:
Reincarnation is a non-Christian doctrine which is often confused with resurrection. In reincarnation, the spirit is continuously born into a new physical form until the spirit learns its lessons and becomes enlightened. The form of reincarnation is determined by the person's karma and may take many lifetimes. Once enlightened, the spirit of the departed person unites with the divine or cosmic all. Once again there is absolutely no Scriptural support for this doctrine.

Pantheism:
Pantheism is the belief that death does not change a spirit and that what survives after death is the same as before death.

- Those who believe in pantheism think that they are already connected to the divine all. The divine all is sometimes called by the name Brahman and is thought of as an all-inclusive reality that exists before and after death.
- The Asian religions adhere to this doctrine, and for them, death is not real and so has no meaning.

Immortality/Platonism:
Those who believe that the soul survives death, but not the body. The disembodied spirit continues to grow and experience existence in intermediate steps until it reaches a state of enlightenment and union with God.

- Those who hold to immortality do not feel that any given religion is necessary.
- They do not believe that one reaches heaven and a relationship with God only through Christ.
- The only thing that survives is an individual spirit with no body.

## THE CHRISTIAN DOCTRINE:
Christians believe in the doctrine of the resurrection.

- Resurrection means that at death the spirit separates from the body. The spirit is reunited at the end of the world with a new, immortal, and powerful body.
- Upon death, the Christian spirit goes to be with the Lord in heaven until the resurrection takes place.
- The disembodied spirit in heaven does not "sleep" nor is it comatose, but has full consciousness of itself, others in heaven and of God. (Philippians 1:23)
- The resurrection takes place through the exercise of a divine miracle at a time appointed by God.
- The supernatural resurrection of the body is the only life after death doctrine in Scripture.
- Our resurrection is dependent on the promises of Jesus. He promised us immortality, and resurrection if we trust him and place our faith in him.
- Our faith in Jesus dissolves the fear of death. At death, we will be with him, and that is the best of all possible outcomes.

## CONCLUSION:

If you place your faith in Jesus, you will go to heaven after you die. You will also receive your resurrection body and a new and beautiful life. How do you know? Read the promises of Christ, and when the fear of death overwhelms you, speak his promises out loud to rebuke the author of death and rejoice in your future with your Lord and Savior, Jesus Christ.

## NOTES:

# Twenty-Seven

# THE FIRST BANK OF HEAVEN

**T**ext: *²⁰But store your treasures in heaven,* **Matthew 6:20 (NCV)**

*¹⁹"Don't store treasures for yourselves here on earth where moths and rust will destroy them and thieves can break in and steal them. ²⁰But store your treasures in heaven where they cannot be destroyed by moths or rust and where thieves cannot break in and steal them. ²¹Your heart will be where your treasure is.* **Matthew 6:19-21 (NCV)**

## INTRODUCTION:

Many Christians breathed a sigh of relief when they realized that because they believe in Jesus Christ when they die they will enter heaven. The question is what we will find when we get to heaven? We know that heaven is a created dimension in which God lives, and in heaven, we will have a personal, intimate relationship with Jesus much more intense and profound than what we can experience here on earth. For some people that is enough, but Scripture implies that we can gain rewards and then deposit them in heaven and enjoy their benefits. So, it seems to me that if you have been accumulating rewards in heaven, when you get there you will be much more content than those who are not making deposits in heaven's bank. The question you need to ask yourself is how I can earn rewards and treasures in heaven? In other words, do I get rewarded for what I do in life?

## ILLUSTRATION:

You may find it difficult to hear this sermon because the idea of building up treasures in heaven (God's kingdom) is often dismissed. To help you understand, I would like to read to you the following illustration of the significance of our rewards in heaven:

Jerome A. Jochem M.S., M.A.

## GOOD MORNING UP THERE:

The late Harry Rimmer *(1890–1952 - American Evangelist and creationist)* penned the following letter to Charles E. Fuller of the Old-Fashioned Revival Hour (1937 to 1968), shortly before his death.

"Next Sunday you are to talk about heaven. I am interested in that land because I have held a clear title to a bit of property there for over 50 years. I did not buy it. I got it without money and price, but the Donor purchased it for me at a tremendous sacrifice. "I am not holding it for speculation. It is not a vacant lot. For more than half a century I have been sending materials, out of which the greatest Architect of the universe has been building a home for me, which will never need remodeling or repairs because it will suit me perfectly, individually, and will never grow old. "Termites can never undermine its foundation for it rests upon the Rock of Ages. Fire cannot destroy it. Floods cannot wash it away. No lock or bolts will ever be placed upon the doors, for no vicious person can ever enter that land, where my dwelling stands, now almost completed and almost ready for me to enter in and abide in peace eternally, without fear of being rejected. "There is a valley of deep shadow between this place where I live, and that to which I shall journey in a very short time. I cannot reach my home in that city without passing through that valley. But I am not afraid because the best Friend I ever had gone through the same valley long, long ago and drove away all its gloom. He stuck with me through thick and thin since we first became acquainted 55 years ago, and I hold his promise in printed form, never to forsake me or leave me alone. He will be with me as I walk through the valley of the shadow of death, and I shall not lose my way because He is with me. "I hope to hear your sermon on heaven next Sunday, but I have no assurance I shall be able to do so. My ticket to heaven has no date marked for the journey, no return coupon and no permit for baggage. Yes, I am ready to go, and I may not be here while you are talking next Sunday evening, but I will meet you there someday."[2]

---

[2] A Treasury of Bible Illustrations. First Edition, © 1995 by AMG INTERNATIONAL, INC. All Rights Reserved. Electronic Edition STEP Files Copyright © 2005, QuickVerse. All rights reserved.

## REWARDED FOR FAITH:

*I tell you, all those who stand before others and say they believe in me, I, the Son of Man, will say before the angels of God that they belong to me.* **Luke 12:8 (NCV)**

- As a reward, you will find that heaven is not a lonely place.
- Every one of your previous relatives who believed in the Lord Jesus Christ is waiting for you to arrive. When you get there, you will be surrounded by generations of family members. Keep in mind that heaven is full of families.
- Your relatives, friends, and church family are also there. Every brother and sister in Christ who you knew, will also be there to celebrate with you.
- Of highest importance, Jesus Christ will identify you as belonging to him. He will declare to everyone who does not know you in heaven, that you are his and he is yours.

## REWARDED FOR SACRIFICE:

*21Jesus, looking at the man, loved him and said," There is one more thing you need to do. Go and sell everything you have, and give the money to the poor, and you will have treasure in heaven. Then come and follow me."* **Mark 10:21 (NCV)**

- Jesus is implying here that we should not hold back anything from him.
- He is also telling us that the most significant treasure on earth cannot compare to the smallest treasure in heaven.
- Notice, however, that making a sacrifice should be followed by obedience to his will, and by establishing a personal relationship with him. *22 But Samuel answered, "What pleases the LORD more: burnt offerings and sacrifices or obedience to his voice? It is better to obey than to sacrifice. It is better to listen to God than to offer the fat of sheep.* **1 Samuel 15:22 (NCV)**

## REWARDED FOR ENDURANCE:

*22People will hate you, shut you out, insult you, and say you are evil because you follow the Son of Man. But when they do, you will be happy. 23Be full of joy at that time, because you have a great reward waiting for you in heaven. Their ancestors did the same things to the prophets.* **Luke 6:22-23 (NCV)**

- At this point in history, the persecution of Christians is at an all-time high. Christians are horrendously tortured and murdered at the hands of the terrorists, and in those nations whose governments are atheistic or Islamic. As Jesus said, *"people will hate you."* (Vs. 22)
- Christians who endure this time of persecution by remaining faithful to Jesus, receive a reward in heaven.
- Notice that in this Scripture, Jesus said that the reward in heaven would be "great" (plenteous, or abundant). Therefore, endurance brings about a great reward, but that reward may not be visible on the earth but is waiting for you in heaven.

## Rewarded for Love:

*34Then the King will say to the people on his right, 'Come, my Father has given you his blessing. Receive the kingdom God has prepared for you since the world was made.35I was hungry, and you gave me food. I was thirsty, and you gave me something to drink. I was alone and away from home, and you invited me into your house. 36I was without clothes, and you gave me something to wear. I was sick, and you cared for me. I was in prison, and you visited me.'* **Matthew 25:34 -36 (NCV)**

In this Scripture portion, Jesus told us six actions or works we need to do to deposit treasure in heaven: I summarized them as follows:

1. Hungry and you gave me food.
2. Thirsty and you gave me drink.
3. Alone and away from home and you invited me into your home.
4. I was without clothes, and you gave me something to wear.
5. I was sick, and you cared for me.
6. I was in prison, and you visited me.

Each one of these works is an expression of selfless love defined in the Bible as "Agape" love.

- We do these things not out of obligation, but because we are expressing the love of Christ to those in need.
- These are also sacrificial actions or works because they demand that we give our resources (time and money) to do the tasks that bring the reward.
- These works are for the entire church because every individual in the church can become involved with them. This means that

each person can have a specific role in these works, from giving money to support the ministry to handing out food or clothes.

- In some cases, these works can be complicated, for example, sitting with a person who is dying and praying with and for that person.
- Some of these works simply demand hospitality, a selfless caring for the welfare of strangers and others who need support.
- These are general works, and every Christian can earn rewards in heaven by doing these kinds of ministries. A special calling is not always necessary, and the lack of a calling is not an excuse for not ministering in these areas.

## LOVE YOUR ENEMIES:

*But love your enemies, do good to them, and lend to them without hoping to get anything back. Then you will have a great reward, and you will be children of the Most High God, because he is kind even to people who are ungrateful and full of sin.* **Luke 6:35 (NCV)**

- Note this is the second verse in which Jesus said you would receive a great reward if you obey his command to love your enemies.
- His specific command was to do "good" to those who would harm you or your family.
- If you do good to your enemy, you are following in the footsteps of God himself, who sent his only begotten Son to bring salvation to those who openly declared God to be their enemy.
- If you follow through with this command, you qualify yourself to be a child of the highest God and will be recognized as such, as a reward in heaven, and even possibly on the earth.
- Our natural tendency, or fleshy tendency, is to strike back aggressively against those who do us harm or desire to do us damage. Therefore, to find a way to love your enemy is a significant challenge, perhaps impossible for human nature. We need God to help us to love anyone but especially our enemies.

## CONCLUSION:

If you listened to what I said, then you are beginning to wonder how much treasure you have deposited in the first bank of Heaven. That's a serious question because one day you're going there to take up residence on the property that God has promised you because you believe in the Lord Jesus Christ as your Lord and Savior. It's never too late to start; it will take effort, work, endurance, and perseverance. It is the purpose of the church to help you do these things, all you need to do is get involved, and if you are involved, you will be blessed with rewards in heaven.

NOTES:

# Twenty-Eight

# THE FIRST WORDS OF THE RESURRECTED JESUS

**T**ext *¹⁰ Then the disciples went back to their homes, ¹¹ but Mary stood outside the tomb crying. As she wept, she bent over to look into the tomb ¹² and saw two angels in white, seated where Jesus' body had been, one at the head and the other at the foot. ¹³ They asked her, "Woman, why are you crying?" "They have taken my Lord away," she said, "and I don't know where they have put him." ¹⁴ At this, she turned around and saw Jesus standing there, but she did not realize that it was Jesus. ¹⁵ "Woman," he said, "why are you crying? Who is it you are looking for?" Thinking he was the gardener, she said, "Sir, if you have carried him away, tell me where you have put him, and I will get him." ¹⁶ Jesus said to her, "Mary." She turned toward him and cried out in Aramaic, "Rabboni!" (which means Teacher). ¹⁷ Jesus said, "Do not hold on to me, for I have not yet returned to the Father. Go instead to my brothers and tell them, 'I am returning to my Father and your Father, to my God and your God.'" ¹⁸ Mary Magdalene went to the disciples with the news: "I have seen the Lord!" And she told them that he had said these things to her. ¹⁹ On the evening of that first day of the week, when the disciples were together, with the doors locked for fear of the Jews, Jesus came and stood among them and said, "Peace be with you!" ²⁰ After he said this, he showed them his hands and side. The disciples were overjoyed when they saw the Lord. ²¹ Again Jesus said, "Peace be with you! As the Father has sent me, I am sending you." ²² And with that he breathed on them and said, "Receive the Holy Spirit. ²³ If you forgive anyone his sins, they are forgiven; if you do not forgive them, they are not forgiven." ²⁴ Now Thomas (called Didymus), one of the Twelve, was not with the disciples when Jesus came. ²⁵ So the other* *disciples told him, "We have seen the Lord!" But he said to them, "Unless I see the nail marks in his hands and put my finger where the nails were, and put my hand into his side, I will not believe it." ²⁶ A week later his disciples were in the house again, and Thomas was with them. Though the doors were locked, Jesus came and stood among them and said, "Peace be with you!" ²⁷ Then he said to Thomas, "Put your finger here; see my hands. Reach out your hand and put it into my side. Stop doubting and believe." ²⁸ Thomas said to him, "My Lord and my God!" ²⁹ Then Jesus told him, "Because you have seen me, you have believed; blessed are those who have not seen and yet have believed."* **John 20:10-29 (NIV)**

## INTRODUCTION:

The work of Christ was not finished after his resurrection. He had the tough task of convincing his disciples and followers that he still lived. Some of his initial contacts and what he said to them is extremely important for our understanding of his intentions and plans. In this sermon, I would like to look at the first three contacts he had with his followers all of which are found in the 20ᵗʰ Chapter of the Book of John.

## JESUS AND MARY MAGDALENE:

*Vs. 10 – 14:* Mary felt intense grief. People who are grieving do not function well, many cases their functioning can drop to as low as 20% below normal.

- The fact that the apostles went home and yet Mary remained weeping before the tomb shows that Mary had a profound emotional attachment to the Lord.
- This attachment is understandable because Jesus delivered her from seven demons which must have made her life very difficult.
- At this point, Mary suffered two losses. The first loss took place when Jesus died, and the second loss took place when his body was missing. The double loss produces double grief.
- Remember that when there is great love, there is also great grief when that love is lost.

*Vs. 15 – 16:* In these verses, we see two contrasting ways in which Jesus approached Mary

- In the first approach, he was remote and asked a question that any stranger would ask a woman is crying and weeping before him. Mary did not recognize Jesus because, in her mind, he was dead and couldn't possibly be standing in front of her alive and well.

- In the second approach, Jesus simply spoke her name. He spoke her name in a way which he had done so before and implied intimacy of a close friendship.
- When Jesus spoke her name, Mary instantly recognized him, and her grief turned to joy. As there was overwhelming grief initially, with the recognition that he was alive, there came an overwhelming joy.
- The significance for us is that one-day Jesus will call us by name and we will enter eternal life with new resurrection bodies and experience that same overwhelming joy. *² The one who enters by the door is the shepherd of the sheep. ³ The one who guards the door, opens it for him. And the sheep listen to the voice of the shepherd. He calls his own sheep by name and leads them out. ⁴ When he brings all his sheep out, he goes ahead of them, and they follow him because they know his voice.* **John 10:2-4 (NCV)**

*Vs. 17 – 18:* Mary responded to the joy she was feeling by running over to Jesus and hugging him and holding on to him never wanting to suffer his loss again.

- Jesus asked Mary not to hold on to him because he had not returned to the Father, and this is both an amazing and beautiful statement.
- It is amazing and beautiful because instead of entering directly into glory with his Father, Jesus waited to make sure that his apostles and disciples knew that he is resurrected and that he would meet them soon.
- Once again, we see Jesus loving his own with real agape love, putting his glory behind the care of his followers. What an excellent example of love.

## JESUS AND THE DISCIPLES:
This meeting took place on the first Sunday mentioned in the Bible.

*Vs. 19 – 20:* The apostles didn't believe the report of Mary Magdalene, and they were huddled together behind locked doors, in fear of persecution by the Jews.

- Jesus somehow entered the room and greeted them with the words "peace be with you" which is the word "Shalom."
- Jesus verified his identity by showing them the marks in his hands and feet, the apostles recognized him, and their intense grief immediately turned to joy.
- Notice the difference between the triggers for Mary and the apostles. For Mary, the trigger was her name and relationship to Christ, for the apostles it was his wounds signifying his work on the cross.

*Vs. 21 – 23:* Once the apostles recognized who he was, he commissioned them in two crucial ways.

1. He sent them into the world to preach the gospel and bring salvation to men in the same way that the Father of Jesus sent his son into the world to save it. The primary function of the apostles and the church today is to follow the pattern of Jesus to bring salvation to the lost.
2. He then authorized them or empowered them to forgive sins in his name, so that men could be freed from the bondage and slavery to sin through the work of the cross. Notice the juxtaposition of Jesus revealing himself through his wounds and his commission to preach the gospel.

*Vs. 21* Special Note:
In this verse, Jesus breathed on his apostles after he commissioned them and said that they are to receive the Holy Spirit.

- In this situation, the apostles receiving the Holy Spirit is not to be confused with the Baptism of the Holy Spirit which was to take place later after Jesus ascended.
- Every Christian receives the Holy Spirit within them. For the apostles receiving the Holy Spirit was part of the regeneration, that is, they became new people as a new creation in Christ.
- Because this happens before Pentecost, the Baptism of the Holy Spirit must be considered a second experience which empowers the spiritual gifts used as tools for witnessing about salvation.

## JESUS AND THOMAS:

Thomas represents those people who do not want to be deceived and want the truth. In this case

*Vs. 24 – 25:* Thomas needed the physical evidence of the wounds of Christ to believe that Jesus had risen.

- There's a lot of people that require proof about Jesus, and like Thomas, they require a particular kind of evidence.
- In Thomas's case, he needed to see the wounds of the crucifixion to be certain that it was, in fact, Jesus who was resurrected and not some imposter.
- Thomas required proof because he loved Jesus and would not accept the possibility of deception.

*Vs. 26 – 28:* People who demand evidence before they can believe in Jesus must be sure to keep their minds open, and they must be willing to accept the evidence that Jesus will provide.

- If, however, they reject the evidence that Jesus provides then they will never come to faith.
- The evidence is supportive, but it is faith that is the final goal.
- In this case, Thomas could get the evidence that his skeptical mind required and it resulted in an immediate increase in his faith that Jesus was Lord and God.

## CONCLUSION:

In Vs. 29, Jesus tells us that we are blessed if we believe without proof. And yet, for most Christians, the presence of Christ in our lives is proof enough. His wounds signify his victory on our behalf over bondage and enslavement to sin. It is, however, his love when he calls us by name that convinces us that he is our Lord and our God.

## NOTES:

# *Twenty-Nine*

# WHY ATTEND CHURCH

**T**ext: *²⁴Let us think about each other and help each other to show love and do good deeds. ²⁵You should not stay away from the church meetings, as some are doing, but you should meet together and encourage each other. Do this even more as you see the day coming.* **Hebrews 10:24-25 (NCV)**

*⁴Each one of us has a body with many parts, and these parts all have different uses.⁵In the same way, we are many, but in Christ we are all one body. Each one is a part of that body, and each part belongs to all the other parts.⁶We all have different gifts, each of which came because of the grace God gave us. The person who has the gift of prophecy should use that gift in agreement with the faith.⁷Anyone who has the gift of serving should serve. Anyone who has the gift of teaching should teach.⁸Whoever has the gift of encouraging others should encourage. Whoever has the gift of giving to others should give freely. Anyone who has the gift of being a leader should try hard when he leads. Whoever has the gift of showing mercy to others should do so with joy.* **Romans 12:4-5 (NCV)**

## INTRODUCTION:

It is very puzzling when you talk to a Christian who believes in the Lord Jesus Christ but does not attend church or will not become a member of the church. These people give you a wide variety of reasons for believing in Christ, but not being involved with his body. In this sermon, I would like to explore why people will not join a church or why they will leave a church.

## THREE REASONS FOR NOT ATTENDING A CHURCH:

The reasons why people will avoid church may be personal, theological, or worldly.

1. Personal Reasons: Many people will leave the church if they have been offended and that offense remains unresolved. Feelings of rejection set in and the person may respond by rejecting the church. Offenses produce feelings of anger. If a person is not able to approach the one who offended him and resolve his antagonism, then his anger will drive him to reject that person. If others criticize him because he is not perfect or in some way deviates from what they expect Christians to be, the criticized person may reject the church by justifying his decision to leave because of the "hypocrisy" and lack of love in the church. Without appropriate resolution, such offenses and the consequential feelings about the church can last for years, and the person may never return to any church.

2. Theological reasons: Many people just do not understand the benefits of the church and how they will spiritually mature as members. In other words, they see no need for church attendance or membership. This seems to be especially true for younger Christians, who think that the church cannot address the problems and difficulties of modern culture and lifestyles. In the eyes of the younger Christians, the church is antiquated and outdated.

3. Worldly reasons: People who do not attend church may be too busy with mundane endeavors (such as sports). They prioritize the church at the lowest level while prioritizing worldly activities higher than attending a church. To put it bluntly, they are too busy and too preoccupied to attend to their spiritual needs. They may also excuse themselves from church attendance by adopting a religious attitude that does not make demands on their time, money, and personal involvement but which does make them feel good about themselves.

## REASONS TO ATTEND:

Ironically, the reasons to attend and become a member of the church are similar to the reasons given by people who do not attend church.

- Personal Reasons: It goes without saying that there will always be someone in a church body that will be offensive. The offense may be purposeful, accidental, or unintentional. Regardless of the nature of the offense, the response must be to resolve the issue. Addressing the issue may demand that we learn how to communicate and to apply the principles of forgiveness to the offender. In no way does the Lord want anyone to withdraw from the church because of offense or feelings of rejection by the church. Our first text tells us that we are to encourage each other and when we do that, we become wiser, smarter, and more mature Christians.

- Theological Reasons: Every Christian is needed in the church because all together we compose the body of Christ. Since each Christian is part of the body, everyone is necessary and if Christians do not attend or become members than something vital is missing in the church. The church is also a support group that will help its members through difficult times with love and understanding. The church is a place designed by the Lord to help mature Christians because through the church you can serve the Lord and develop a love for others.

- Worldly Reasons: If a person is so involved with secular activities that there is no time for church, then that person will starve his spirit and weaken his faith. The church is a place that the human soul gets nourished by the Word of God. It is within the church that the Word is heard and faith is made strong. As a person ignores spiritual needs, the grip of the world becomes stronger, and soon that person is Christian in name only. The worldly things are temporary, and the things of the spirit are eternal, yet many who refuse to belong to the body of Christ are investing in the temporary and rejecting the eternal, and that is a tragic mistake.

## CONCLUSION:

If you know a person who says that he is a Christian, encourage him to come to the church and grow in the Lord. Tell him that the church needs him, and while he is not obligated to join, he should visit and hear from the Lord. Even if he does not decide to go to your church and if he begins to attend a different church, then you have supported him and pleased the Lord. Give answers to accusations against the church and no matter what his attitude may be, love him!

NOTES:

# Thirty

# THE SEED OF GOD'S KINGDOM

**T**ext: *³⁰Then Jesus said, "How can I show you what the kingdom of God is like? What story can I use to explain it? ³¹The kingdom of God is like a mustard seed, the smallest seed you plant in the ground. ³²But when planted, this seed grows and becomes the largest of all garden plants. It produces large branches, and the wild birds can make nests in its shade."* **Mark 4:30-32 (NCV)**

## INTRODUCTION:

It is clear from Scripture that there are two kingdoms to which we can belong. The first is the kingdom of God, and the second is the kingdom of Satan. Scripture symbolized these kingdoms as that of light and darkness.

- The kingdom of God reflects all the sweet features of God. These features include love, mercy, kindness, joy, peace, and holiness.
- The kingdom of Satan mirrors the nature of Satan and so consists of perversions of God's kingdom such as hatred, sickness, fear, terror, cruelty, abuse, murder, and spiritual deception. These things are commonly called evil, and so Satan's kingdom is one of real spiritual darkness.
- Even though the two kingdoms could not be any more dissimilar from each other, they both grow through the same process which is the setting of a "seed."
- As Christians, it's our duty and our privilege to plant the seeds of the kingdom of Heaven in humanity. Each of us must become "seed planters" so that others can reap the crop, and the kingdom of God can grow everywhere in the world.

- However, to plant seeds effectively, we must know what we are doing and how to do it. Jesus gave us guidance in several stories that he told us.

## THE CONDITION OF THE HEART:

*³Then Jesus used stories to teach them many things. He said: "A farmer went out to plant his seed. ⁴While he was planting, some seed fell by the road, and the birds came and ate it all up. ⁵Some seed fell on rocky ground, where there wasn't much dirt. That seed grew very fast, because the ground was not deep. ⁶But when the sun rose, the plants dried up, because they did not have deep roots. ⁷Some other seed fell among thorny weeds, which grew and choked the good plants. ⁸Some other seed fell on good ground where it grew and produced a crop. Some plants made a hundred times more, some made sixty times more, and some made thirty times more. ⁹You people who can hear me, listen."* **Matthew 13:3-9 (NCV)**

In this Scripture, Jesus told us that the effect of planting a seed depends on the heart condition of the people who receive it. He gave us four conditions that govern the outcome of sowing the seeds of the kingdom of God.

## A LACK OF UNDERSTANDING:

*¹⁸"So listen to the meaning of that story about the farmer. ¹⁹What is the seed that fell by the road? That seed is like the person who hears the message about the kingdom but does not understand it. The Evil One comes and takes away what was planted in that person's heart.* **Matthew 13:18-19 (NCV)**

- It is evident from this passage that Satan can enter the heart of someone who has heard the Gospel and steal the seed of salvation that was planted there by our witness.
- This happens, however, because of a lack of understanding about what it means to be saved and a member of God's kingdom.

It is very clear from this passage that if we are to plant the seeds of the kingdom of God effectively, then we must make sure we do so in a way that communicates understanding as well as acceptance. In other words, an altar call will be ineffective if the people who are responding remain ignorant of what they are doing. It is our responsibility to make sure they understand what the call means. We must plant the seed of knowledge and discipleship.

## A LACK OF PASSION:

*²⁰And what is the seed that fell on rocky ground? That seed is like the person who hears the teaching and quickly accepts it with joy. ²¹But he does not let the teaching go deep into his life, so he keeps it only a short time. When trouble or persecution comes because of the teaching he accepted, he quickly gives up.* **Matthew 13:20-21 (NCV)**

- The problem here is not a lack of understanding, but a lack of passion.
- The heart is resistant to the seed because of two underlying reasons.
    1. First, the person has a contented and comfortable life full of riches and blessings. He thinks that he doesn't need Christ.
    2. Second, his heart is so troubled, and life is so turbulent that he thinks Christ can't help him overcome his problems. Once again, he thinks he doesn't need Christ.

To be effective seed planters with this type of person, we must take time to establish a relationship with the person so that during tough times we can show him how Christ can help him overcome. It is a sure bet that hard times will come, but it is equally certain that this type of person can find a need for Christ regardless of his circumstances.

## A LACK OF FAITH:

*²²And what is the seed that fell among the thorny weeds? That seed is like the person who hears the teaching, but lets worry about this life and the temptation of wealth stop that teaching from growing. So, the teaching does not produce fruit in that person's life.* **Matthew 13:22 (NCV)**

- The problem here is not a lack of understanding or passion, but a lack of trust and faith in God.
- This type of person may be the most common type with which we must deal as seed planters.
- Our society is one of fear, and that fear seems to be growing with each year that passes. We are continually talking about the economy (strong or weak) or the need for financial help from the government.

- When these persons begin to see security in wealth, they become deceived and will make decisions to increase their wealth in the world rather than their wealth in the kingdom of God.
- His anxiety, worry, and fear became a curse, and he never matures into the fruit of the Spirit. Not at least until he reaches a breaking point and begins to see that God is his provider.

To be effective seed planters with this type of person, we must help him experience the true and the commanding presence and power of God through the manifestations of Christ by the Holy Spirit. It is not until he knows that he can trust God to provide and take care of his fears and worries that the seed will grow and mature.

## Fruit Bearer:

*²³But what is the seed that fell on the good ground? That seed is like the person who hears the teaching and understands it. That person grows and produces fruit, sometimes a hundred times more, sometimes sixty times more, and sometimes thirty times more."* **Matthew 13:23(NCV)**

- This is only one out of every four people in which we attempt to plant the seed.
- The key for these people is that they hear the Word and develop faith and trust in the Lord and that they understand what they know so they can apply it to their lives.
- When they apply the Word to their lives with trust in God, they begin to grow and produce fruit.
- The first kind of fruit they produce is the fruit of the Holy Spirit that is internal and personal to their lives. With the development of this fruit, they can defeat Satan's attempts to steal them from Christ.
- The second kind of fruit results from the seeds they plant in others to expand the kingdom of God. There are variations in the amount of fruit, but that is explained by their degree of passion for planting seeds.

## Conclusion:

The kingdom of darkness has been spreading and growing through hate and violence. Rather than despairing about this, we should become even more determined to plant the seeds of the kingdom of God. The light will overcome the darkness so we will see others enter the kingdom

Jerome A. Jochem M.S., M.A.

of light as we witness to them and plant the seeds of faith, trust, and submission to God. Remember that you are God's seed planter and do what you must to expand his kingdom.

NOTES:

# Thirty-One

## THE TRANSFIGURATION
## AND THE GLORY

**T**ext: *²⁹While Jesus was praying, the appearance of his face changed, and his clothes became shining white. ³⁰Then two men, Moses and Elijah were talking with Jesus. ³¹They appeared in heavenly glory, talking about his departure which he would soon bring about in Jerusalem.* **Luke 9:29-31 (NCV)**

### INTRODUCTION:
Among certain Christian churches, the emphasis is placed on "entering into the glory" of God. Entire sermons preach about the manifestation of God's glory during the service. In some sermons I have heard, glory is treated as a state of being which is different than being anointed with God's power as followers of Christ. The question is what is the Biblical glory of God and can we expect to experience it?

### FACTS ABOUT THE GLORY:
There are several words used in both the Old and New Testaments translated as glory in the English versions of the Bible.

- In the Old Testament, about seven words are translated as glory in the various English versions. One thing they all have in common is they mean brightness, light, rare, beautiful, and desirable.
- These words tend to communicate the idea of a particular event which is of great beauty, majesty and splendor predominantly applied to external things or even men. For example, kings have

the glory that may consist of wealth, power, dignity or inherent majesty.

- However, most commonly, God's glory is seen in his power and divine character. This glory is attributed to him or to anything connected to him, including his people, the temple, and includes his judgments. The glory of his judgments is expressed through catastrophic events like earthquakes, and volcanoes. (Isaiah 2, 19, 21).

- One word in the Old Testament, "Kabhodh," means "weight," "heaviness," seems to convey the idea of some external and physical manifestation of dignity, preeminence or majesty. In this usage, the word describes the form in which God reveals himself or is the sign of the manifestation of his presence.

- The word in the New Testament translated as glory is "Doxa "and also carries with it the sense of brightness, brilliance, splendor which is either natural or supernatural as in the case of Paul's experience on the road to Damascus.

## THE APOSTLES AND CHRIST'S GLORY:

This experience probably took place in Caesarea Philippi, on the highest mountain in the area which is Mount Herman. This mountain is referred to as the "high mountain" in Matthew 17 and Mark 9. Three things of great significance happened before the Transfiguration.

1.  Peter made his great confession when Christ asked him *"Who do you say I am?"* **Matthew 16:15 (NIV)** and then Peter recognizes Christ as the son of the living God. (Matthew 16:16).
2.  Jesus then predicted his death and resurrection. (Matthew 16:21–27).
3.  Peter was shocked and objected to Jesus's death, and Jesus rebuked Peter because of Peter's denial of God's sovereignty. (Matthew 16:23).

These three events prepared the ground for the revelation of Christ's glory during the Transfiguration.

In the same way, God will prepare us for the manifestation of his glory as we continue to worship him, submit to his sovereignty, and walk with his Spirit daily.

## THE EVENT OF THE TRANSFIGURATION:

*Vs. 28:* The transfiguration begins with prayer.

- The Greek indicates that this was not just a routine prayer meeting but was something special. Jesus took his disciples up the high mountain for a specific purpose, and that was to show them his glory

- In the same way, Jesus will take us into his glory as long as we follow him and maintain our expectation that he will reveal himself to us.

*Vs. 29:* In the Book of Mark, Chapter 9, the word "transfigured" in Greek gives us our English word "metamorphosis," and it means that Jesus changed on a fundamental level. This change was from the inside out, and it occurred during the time that Christ was praying or talking to his Father.

- In Vs. 29 we also see the emphasis on brightness, dazzling white, all of which were used for God's glory throughout the Bible.

- Also, note that in Vs. 29 the appearance of his face changed, the Greek word means that his face became perceptibly different than his normal appearance and implied that his glory was that of the king of heaven and earth.

*Vs. 30:* At this point, two Old Testament personalities appeared with Christ in his glory. The first was Moses and the second was Elijah. These two men represent two groups of believers.

- Moses died, and therefore he represents those who will die in the Lord and be raised to meet with Christ at his return.

- Elijah did not die but was taken up into heaven (2 Kings 2:1), and he represents those who will be alive at the second coming and will be changed. (1 Corinthians 15:51 – 52).

*Vs. 34:* Clouds, thunderstorms, and smoke are frequently associated with the glory of God in the Old Testament. (Deuteronomy 5:24, 2 Chronicles 7:1-3).

- Here we see God the Father expressing his glory to affirm the glory of Jesus.

- The purpose of this manifestation of God's glory was to instruct the apostles to listen to and therefore continue to follow Jesus as he begins his voyage to the cross.

- In the same way, God the Father wants us to follow Jesus to our cross and will manifest his glory to instruct and strengthen us.

Jerome A. Jochem M.S., M.A.

## CONCLUSION:

The glory of God is an intense manifestation of his presence. Sometimes that event takes the form of holiness, judgment, power, or some other fundamental characteristic of God. Just as he showed us his glory in the past, there is no reason for us to think that he will not reveal his glory to us today and in the future. When God manifests his glory, there is always a purpose for him to do so. In this case, the Transfiguration of Christ revealed his glory as the King of Kings and was a glimpse into the coming kingdom of God which we all await.

## NOTES:

# FOUNDATIONS

**Thirty-Two**

**Text:** [46]*"Why do you call me, 'Lord, Lord,' but do not do what I say? [47]I will show you what everyone is like who comes to me and hears my words and obeys. [48]That person is like a man building a house who dug deep and laid the foundation on rock. When the floods came, the water tried to wash the house away, but it could not shake it, because the house was built well. [49]But the one who hears my words and does not obey is like a man who built his house on the ground without a foundation. When the floods came, the house quickly fell and was completely destroyed."* **Luke 6:46-49 (NCV)**

## INTRODUCTION:

Faith and trust in Jesus are something that we build as we mature in our Christian walk. Of vital importance is that we create that faith on solid foundations. In our text, Jesus said that we have a choice about the foundation upon which we rest our faith. Our option is to build a strong foundation based on obedience or a weak foundation based on disobedience and neglect of the Word. In this sermon, I would like to explore both foundations and how we can build a strong foundation to stay strong in our faith in Jesus.

## A WEAK FOUNDATION:

A weak foundation results from these factors:

- Over time we all tend to make our foundations from our blessings.
- We may not even be aware that we have moved our faith onto shifting sands.

- God will undoubtedly test our foundations and show us that a weak foundation can bring destruction to our faith!
- What we do when the flood comes will determine our relationship and commitment to God and Jesus Christ.
- Weak foundations tend to be about future events which are in some way dependent upon our present actions and level of faith.
- They are based on false hope rather than the established Word.
- They may produce only temporary consequences and benefits.

## WEAK FOUNDATIONS DEPEND ON SIGNS:

*Jesus sighed deeply and said, "Why do you people ask for a miracle as a sign? I tell you the truth, no sign will be given to you. "* **Mark 8:12 (NCV)**

The word "sign" is used by Jesus to denote miraculous and supernatural works of Godly power. His response was to the demand that he prove he is the Son of God by performing such works.

- Jesus has no problem performing many miracles as signs that pointed to his divine nature.
- In this situation, the people did not have faith in him, and they wanted a miracle so they could believe.
- Their focus was on the miracle not on the person who is their savior.
- This is a traditional example of a weak foundation for faith in Christ.
- Notice that he challenged them to believe without a sign.

## EXAMPLES OF WEAK FOUNDATIONS:

What we believe and the reason we believe it both determine the strength of our foundation. We may have faith but for the wrong reason. When that reason is not supported, then our faith diminishes. Some examples of such weak foundations include the following:

- Demand for healing. Believe because you need to be healed and not because God is a healing God.
- Answered prayer. Believe because God will always grant your prayers. No response or a negative response leads to diminished faith.
- Prosperity. Believe because of a desire to get rich through faith in Christ.

- Spiritual gifts. Believe to get personal spiritual power.
- The glory of God. Believe only if directly experienced.

## THE ONLY STRONG FOUNDATION:
*²I decided that while I was with you I would forget about everything except Jesus Christ and his death on the cross.* **1 Corinthians 2:2 (NCV)**

Our only sure foundation on which to base our faith in Jesus Christ and the work he did on the cross. When we stand on that foundation, our faith cannot be weakened or shaken by a lack of a "sign" or by rejection and persecution. There are several reasons that he is our sure and steady foundation:

- He is a real historical person. Not a fable nor an expectation, but his existence is an indisputable fact.
- He completed his work on the cross for us. It did not depend on our opinion or actions. The cross is the harsh reality of his sacrifice for those who believe after the fact.
- He was resurrected, which means that for those who follow him, he is a concrete reality today. He is with us, in us, and on us!
- He does not fail us, abandon us, nor is he limited by our faith. He is the Almighty God.

## CONCLUSION:
Self-examination is required if we are to determine how strong a foundation we hold to in this troubled world. We need to be sure that we are not clinging to temporary experiences and making them the foundation for what we believe. The person of Jesus, his commandments, his promises, his love for us are the pillars which give us a strong foundation. If we always keep him as our foundation, we shall not be shaken.

## NOTES:

# DECISION TIME

**T**ext: *²⁴It was by faith that Moses, when he grew up, refused to be called the son of the king of Egypt's daughter. ²⁵He chose to suffer with God's people instead of enjoying sin for a short time. ²⁶He thought it was better to suffer for the Christ than to have all the treasures of Egypt, because he was looking for God's reward. ²⁷Moses continued strong as if he could see the God that no one can see. ²⁸It was by faith that Moses prepared the Passover and spread the blood on the doors so the one who brings death would not kill the firstborn sons of Israel.* **Hebrews 11:24-28 (NCV)**

## INTRODUCTION:

The Book of Genesis tells us that we are made in the image of God. Among other things, that means is we have free will. Since we have free will, we can choose between different situations. When we exercise this power of choice, we make a decision. Our whole life consists of decisions, some small, some large, that have profound effects on our destiny. To grow as a Christian, we must make the right decisions. The question is how do you make good decisions?

## CHOOSE GOD'S PLAN:

Moses was looking for God's reward instead of his personal pleasures. He could have lived a life of luxury and decadence but chose instead to identify with God's people who were slaves.

Moses came to a decision, and all of us should come to the same decision as well. Moses selected God's plan in his life rather than his plan.

- Sometimes it is difficult for us to give up the idea that we are the captain of our destiny. It takes a certain amount of humility to accept God's plan in our life.
- After you humble yourself before the Lord and accept his plan, then you must follow through and do what he wants you to do no matter how complex or extraordinary that is.
- Remember, it may take determination and courage to follow God's plan in your life.

## Choose Authenticity:

Being authentic just means being true to yourself. The question is who are you spiritually?

- Moses, from a worldly perspective, seemed to be giving up everything that the world thinks is valuable. He was more than willing to identify with slaves rather than the royal family.
- Remember that the things that count greatly in this world are of little concern to God. God is not impressed with what we have but is most concerned with who we are in relationship to him.
- The world will try to force you to make decisions that conform to its values and desires, but that which should govern our choices is our identity in Christ. We must make decisions that strengthen and explore our character. Ultimately, we all must settle the question of our identity. Who are we? The answer is that we are God's

## Choose Self-Denial:

If you are a born again and Spirit-filled Christian you do not fall into sin. You do not slip and slide into immorality. You decide to sin, even when you know that such a decision will displease the Lord and harm yourself and others.

- Just as we can decide to sin, we can also choose not to sin. Yes, sin is fun, but it is always followed by a price we pay later. In every case, the price we pay is not fun at all and may bring destruction to our lives.
- The decision to sin is often the path of least resistance, but that path is always a dangerous road.

- To grow spiritually, you must choose self-denial otherwise the inability to say no to what is sinful and dishonorable can ruin your life.

## Choose Heavenly Awards:

Because Moses was a member of Pharaoh's household, he would have all the riches a man could ever want.

- If Moses had decided to worship the gods of Egypt, he would have been buried in a magnificent pyramid tomb surrounded by all his wealth and slaves. Instead, he is buried in an unmarked grave on a lonely hill in the desert.
- Like Moses, to grow spiritually, we must not value earthly wealth and prestige, but we must focus on our rewards in heaven that will last for eternity. Did Moses make the right choice - did he make a right decision?
- The answer is in the fact that God presided at his funeral.

## Conclusion:

It is far better to follow God's plan in your life than ignoring what God wants you to do because you prefer to do what you want to do instead of God's plan. To reject God's plan for your life is to accept the second best instead of the absolute best that you can get out of life. If you do not know what God's plan is for you, then ask, and he will tell you by making your path clear and straight.

## Notes:

# Thirty-Four

# TROUBLED WATERS OF LIFE

**T**ext: *²⁷But Jesus quickly spoke to them, "Have courage! It is I. Do not be afraid." ²⁸Peter said, "Lord, if it is really you, then command me to come to you on the water." ²⁹Jesus said, "Come." And Peter left the boat and walked on the water to Jesus. ³⁰But when Peter saw the wind and the waves, he became afraid and began to sink. He shouted, "Lord, save me!" ³¹Immediately Jesus reached out his hand and caught Peter. Jesus said, "Your faith is small. Why did you doubt?" ³²After they got into the boat, the wind became calm. ³³Then those who were in the boat worshiped Jesus and said, "Truly you are the Son of God!"* **Matthew 14:28-31 (NCV)**

## INTRODUCTION:

This Scripture is a snapshot of our life experience. We will all go through periods of time in our lives that are turbulent and troublesome. This might happen because of our own choices or because of factors beyond our control. The winds of adversity may blow so forcefully that we are surrounded by chaos and turmoil. The Scripture quoted above gives us a solution to how we are to find peace and tranquility in troubled waters. I'd like to examine some of the crucial points illustrated by this Scripture.

## PETER'S FOUR DECISIONS:

1. Peter's first decision had to do with the fact that he was out in a boat amid high waves in a tempestuous wind not as a matter of choice but of obedience. In the same manner, we often find ourselves facing trials and tribulations that come upon us not by our choice but by the way life treats us. Ultimately, though,

he did what Jesus commanded him to do and ended up facing danger.

2. Peter's second decision was to step out of the boat into the water. He wanted to walk on water which was blatantly impossible for him, and so he had to start with an initial faith in Christ. Perhaps the hardest part of making this decision was taking the first step out of the boat. This is also true of us, once we hear what the Lord is commanding us to do, we must gather up the faith to do it or become disobedient and lose the blessing that the Lord has for us.

3. Peter's third decision was to focus on the uproar surrounding him and pay more attention to the wind and the waves than to Jesus. As a result, his faith in Jesus diminished, and he began to sink into the water. This also is true of us when we face a dangerous and frightening situation in our lives. We tend to believe and place our faith in dire predictions and fearful outcomes rather than the Lord.

4. Finally, Peter's last decision was to recognize Jesus as his savior. He cried out to the Lord for help and was not disappointed. In the end, we also must turn to the Lord when we are faced with an impossible, dangerous, and fearful situation. It is true that we will not be disappointed either.

## THE REACTIONS OF JESUS:

One of the most exciting aspects of the above Scripture is Jesus's reaction to Peter's request. Once again, we can learn much about how our Jesus will respond to us because we can see how he responded to Peter:

- The first observation that we should make is that Jesus knew his disciples would run into trouble because of the winds and violent sea. He knows everything because he's omniscient and yet he sent his disciples to face difficult times. In the same way, the Lord knows what is going to happen in our lives and is prepared to be there for us while we face the chaos that life can bring. He knows what we will need before we know it or need it.

- In Vs. 28 Peter said, *"Lord, if it is really you, then command me to come to you on the water."* This sounded to me like a challenge, that is, Peter was challenging Jesus to perform a miracle to prove that he was the Messiah. Jesus decided to comply with Peter's request only because it would build Peter's faith. This is entirely different than merely demanding a sign to confirm unbelief as others had done. While we are walking through difficult times, Christ may ask us to place our faith in who he is because with him all things are possible.

- As soon as Peter's attention was distracted from Jesus, his faith began to weaken, and he started to sink into the sea. He was now facing the fear of drowning in a violent sea. Peter cried out to Jesus for help, and Jesus reacted by reaching out to Peter and supporting him until they return to the boat. From this, we can learn that when we cry out to Jesus in our dismay and fear, he will respond by supporting us and helping us get past the mayhem of our lives.

## FACTS OF FAITH:

[31]*Immediately Jesus reached out his hand and caught Peter. Jesus said, "Your faith is small. Why did you doubt?"*

The phrase *"Your faith is small"* means a lack of trust. Trust and faith are often used interchangeably in Scripture. The following are some critical points about the facts of faith:

- Faith is not measured by quantity. Faith is measured by how much you apply it in your everyday life. Peter had a little faith because it did not extend much beyond the boat. A great faith would be a faith applied to every area of life. If you have little faith, you trust Jesus only in a few things, but if you have great faith, you trust Jesus in everything.
- A lack of faith means that you do not do what God tells you to do. This begins with the assumption that when in doubt you will ask and God will tell you exactly what he wants to be done and how to do it.
- Doing something that God has not told you to do is also a lack of faith. You may have a good idea, but it is not God's idea, and you end up in disobedience and a lack of submission.
- In Peter's case, he was told to walk on water, and he started off doing exactly that, but then his faith did not cover continuing to walk on water as he paid attention to the turbulent winds and seas.

- It's important not to judge others on what we think is the size of their faith. What we see as a lack of faith may be obedience to Christ rather than a refusal to do what God tells that person to do.

## Conclusion:

Despite what life throws at us, or the foolishness of our own choices, our Lord is there for us to help us not only endure but to have the eventual victory. These life catastrophes can be used by Jesus to build our faith and our relationship with him. Please note that after Peter and Jesus had returned to the boat, the winds calmed down and the danger passed. Terrifying and upsetting situations will happen in our lives, but with Jesus on our side, we will make it through to the other side.

## Notes:

# Thirty-Five

## UPDATING THE SPIRITUAL GIFTS

**T**ext: ¹Now, brothers and sisters, I want you to understand about spiritual gifts. **1 Corinthians 12:1 (NCV)**

⁴*There are different kinds of gifts, but they are all from the same Spirit.* ⁵*There are different ways to serve but the same Lord to serve.* ⁶*And there are different ways that God works through people but the same God. God works in all of us in everything we do.* ⁷*Something from the Spirit can be seen in each person, for the common good.* ⁸*The Spirit gives one person the ability to speak with wisdom, and the same Spirit gives another the ability to speak with knowledge.* ⁹*The same Spirit gives faith to one person. And, to another, that one Spirit gives gifts of healing.* ¹⁰*The Spirit gives to another person the power to do miracles, to another the ability to prophesy. And he gives to another the ability to know the difference between good and evil spirits. The Spirit gives one person the ability to speak in different kinds of languages£ and to another the ability to interpret those languages.* ¹¹*One Spirit, the same Spirit, does all these things, and the Spirit decides what to give each person.* **1 Corinthians 12:4-11 (NCV)**.

### INTRODUCTION:

Those of you who are baptized in the Holy Spirit for a long time, probably know this Scripture well. Please do not disregard this sermon because it may contain new insight that will help you function better in the gifts.

- God wants his people to operate in the spiritual gifts with knowledge and not ignorance.
- God has released his divine power through the structure provided by the spiritual gifts.

- The more we know and understand that structure the more we can release God's power.

## ANALYSIS:
*Vs. 4: ⁴There are different kinds of gifts, but they are all from the same Spirit. ⁵There are different ways to serve but the same Lord to serve.*

All the gifts come from God - nothing that you have or know or can do is of the slightest significance to the operation of the gift. The gifts operate through God's power, not your power; therefore, you do not own them. They are not your gifts nor do they belong to you in any manner.

- Owning a gift diminishes God's glory in that gift.
- Owning a gift substitutes yourself for God.
- Owning a gift may destroy the purpose of that gift (to bring the person to God.)

*Vs. 5-6: ⁵There are different ways to serve but the same Lord to serve. ⁶And there are different ways that God works through people but the same God. God works in all of us in everything we do*

- When you operate in a spiritual gift, you are directly serving the Lord.
- Your voice becomes his voice, and your hand becomes his hand.
- Note here that the Lord refers to Jesus.
- So, through any of the gifts, you are serving Jesus, who is the second person of the Trinity.
- God does not restrict his gifts to one gift per person, but a single person can get multiple gifts all from God.
- Note that in this verse the term God references God the Father, the first person of the Trinity.

*Vs. 7: ⁷Something from the Spirit can be seen in each person, for the common good.*

- Each born again and Holy Spirit baptized believer can get something (some gift) from the Holy Spirit.
- A church full of Holy Spirit baptized members should also have Holy Spirit gifts in operation.

- This means that not just one or two members should operate in the gifts, but the majority should be doing so in an orderly manner.
- A healthy church is one in which the gifts are in operation within the church and in the community as well.

*Vs. 8: ⁸The Spirit gives one person the ability to speak with wisdom, and the same Spirit gives another the ability to speak with knowledge*

- The gifts of wisdom and knowledge are the problem-solving gifts.
- The gift of knowledge reveals the problem supernaturally - i.e., information beyond common understanding or logical deduction.
- The gift of wisdom reveals the answer to the problem. It is the supernatural answer to the supernaturally revealed problem.
- Knowledge and wisdom are the essential elements of the productive spirit filled prayer. While praying, both knowledge and wisdom will be released to give direction and effectiveness to the prayer.
- During prayer, the gift of knowledge will allow the prayer to be targeted to an area of need while the gift of wisdom gives direction to resolve the problem or area of need.

*Vs. 9: ⁹The same Spirit gives faith to one person. And, to another, that one Spirit gives gifts of healing*

- The gift of faith and healing are linked power gifts. That is, faith must be present for healing to take place.
- Faith is a gift given in the face of the physically impossible.
- Many times, a request for the gift of faith should happen before asking for the gift of healing.
- The gift of faith is given to either the healer or the one needing healing.
- It does not take great faith for healing. Often just asking for healing is enough to get it.

*Vs. 10: ¹⁰The Spirit gives to another person the power to do miracles, to another the ability to prophesy.*

- Miracles and prophecy are connected because each requires direct action on the part of God.

- Prophecy is now a gift which means that any Spirit-filled Christian can hear from God and give a prophecy.
- Do not confuse Spirit-filled prayer with prophecy. Prophecy is directly hearing a word from God and then delivering that word to people. It is "what the Lord says" not "what I feel about it or what I think."
- The gifts of knowledge and wisdom do not constitute prophecy. Prophecy is listed as a separate gift that requires direct communication with God.

*And he gives to another the ability to know the difference between good and evil spirits.*
- The gift of discernment applies both to the supernatural and natural.
- Discernment can reveal false teachings of a human teacher, and it can expose and strip away the disguise of evil or unclean spirits.
- The gift of discernment is fundamental to a deliverance ministry.

*The Spirit gives one person the ability to speak in different kinds of languages[£] and to another the ability to interpret those languages.*
- Tongues are the battlefield gift because it is often the focus of conflict between Spirit-baptized and other Christians.
- Tongues are the first evidence of the Baptism of the Holy Spirit based on the Biblical pattern shown in the book of Acts.
- Tongues directly attack the ego and self-centeredness of people. As a result, it is rejected.
- Tongues may be the supernatural speaking of a language unknown to the speaker but known to others.
- Tongues may be an unknown language. The spoken language is unknown to those present but exists in some other time or culture.
- Tongues may be the vocalization of supernatural beings such as angels.
- Tongues may constitute a prayer language unknown to the one praying but known by God. As such, it bypasses the limitation of prayer in the person's language.

*Vs. 11: ¹¹One Spirit, the same Spirit, does all these things, and the Spirit decides what to give each person.*

- We can, usually, only receive the spiritual gifts after we have been baptized in the Holy Spirit because it is through the Spirit that the gifts are given and activated.
- Although the Holy Spirit is mentioned, the gifts are given by the full Trinity.
- As a result, the gifts are truly God's gifts and should be sought and not rejected or avoided.
- Being God gifts, they will never harm or do damage to those giving them or those receiving them.

## CONCLUSION:

Knowing that the Spiritual gifts are given to us by a willing and powerful God, we should do our best to operate within the parameters given to us by the Holy Spirit. The gifts are given for the blessing and benefit of the whole church, and the church should both allow and encourage its members to receive the gifts freely and wholeheartedly.

## NOTES:

# Thirty-Six
## WALKING WITH GOD

**T**ext: *²¹When Enoch was 65 years old, he had a son named Methuselah.²²After Methuselah was born, Enoch walked with God 300 years more and had other sons and daughters. ²³So Enoch lived a total of 365 years. ²⁴Enoch walked with God; one-day Enoch could not be found, because God took him.* **Genesis 5:21-24 (NCV)**

*⁵It was by faith that Enoch was taken to heaven so he would not die. He could not be found, because God had taken him away. Before he was taken, the Scripture says that he was a man who truly pleased God. ⁶Without faith no one can please God. Anyone who comes to God must believe that he is real and that he rewards those who truly want to find him.* ***Hebrews 11:5-6 (NIV)***

### INTRODUCTION:
Enoch was amazing because he was the first pre-Christian person to enter heaven and he did it without having to die. The second person to do this was Elijah: (2 Kings 2:11) Hebrews says that God so honored Enoch because in walked with God by faith. Faith means that Enoch first trusted God and demonstrated that trust by depending on him. Enoch showed us that walking with God means that in all matters of life we must trust God and depend on him. But the question is, how do we walk with him? We need to ask what is the foundation of our trust and dependency on God?

### TWO FOUNDATIONAL EXPERIENCES:
To walk with God, we must know something about God and ourselves.

About Ourselves:

We must understand ourselves. We have to have an epiphany of what we need:

- The first part of this knowledge comes from personal desperation that results in insight.
    - o We all live in a world which is neither kind nor gentle.
    - o Devastating events confront us.
    - o We work under the delusion that we are in control until such events show us differently.
    - o They were human beings, so Enoch was no exception to the harshness of life, and neither was Elijah.
- The epiphany that these men must have had was that they needed God.
- They needed him daily and not just in desperate times.
- They developed a consciousness of his presence and lived with him. They walked with him through their lives, and in Enoch's case for 365 years.
- They walked by faith and not in ignorance, but because they knew God intimately and trusted him with all they had and all they were.

About God - a revelation of what God needs:

- The Bible tells us that God is love. (1 John 4:16).
- Love does not exist in a vacuum. If there is one who loves, then there must be a beloved.
- The revelation that Enoch must have had is that God needed Enoch as much as Enoch needed God.
- This applies to you and me as well. Together, we constitute a loving relationship.
- We can conclude that God needs us and we can put our faith in that need because it is essential to the nature of the God who is love.
- We can realize in our walk with God that:
    - o We need God, and he needs us.
    - o Our need is to love God, and his need is to love us.
    - o Our need is to give to God, and his need is to give to us.
    - o Our need is to share ourselves with God, and God's need is to share himself with us.

- o   Our need is to please God, and his need is to bless and reward us.
- o   Our need is to be forgiven, and his need is to forgive us.
- o   Our need is to be free of death, and his need is to give us eternal life.

## Conclusion:

We cannot walk with God unless we have the heart knowledge that we need God to be in every part of our life. We express that heart knowledge in our surrender of our lives in obedience to him. We cannot walk with God in trust or faith unless we have the heart knowledge that he needs to love us and form a relationship with us. We can find peace and faith in knowing and feeling that we are in an unbreakable partnership with God who is our Savior, Father, and Counselor. We can deepen our love as we recognize and meet God's need for our love.

## Notes:

# *Thirty-Seven*
# ADVENTURES WITH GOD

**T**ext: *[16]"God loved the world so much that he gave his one and only Son so that whoever believes in him may not be lost, but have eternal life.* **John 3:16 (NCV)**

## INTRODUCTION:
When you first believe in Christ, fundamental changes occur spiritually and personally, and you are no longer lost but have eternal life. For the first time, real changes happen in your daily life, and that means that what once was impossible becomes possible for you. Life as a Christian becomes an adventure instead of a burden. In this sermon, I would like to discuss four adventures we all share as Christians and all of which relate to eternal life.

## THE ADVENTURE OF THE NEW CREATION:
*[17]If anyone belongs to Christ, there is a new creation. The old things have gone; everything is made new!* **2 Corinthians 5:17 (NCV)**

People who feel condemned under the slavery of sin, and who are suffering from the hurt and pain caused by a sinful lifestyle long for freedom and a new life. When a person makes a commitment to Christ, whose old ways of feeling, thinking, and living, are set aside, and a unique opportunity is given to embrace more of life.
- The new creation is not a matter of transformation but replacement.
- The death of Christ set you free from the slavery of sin, and this results in the ability to choose a different way of living.

- The new creation involves a change that produces a fundamentally different person.
- Salvation reverses some of the old sinful ways, while others take time to change.
- Many times, those reversed immediately have destructive consequences.
- Other sinful behaviors are reverse more slowly as the person struggles to obtain righteousness and holiness in their life.
- The development of the fruit of the Spirit helps this slower reversal process to take place.
- Whether immediately reversed or reversed over time the individual through the new creation is set free to become a different person living a new lifestyle.
- It is imperative that the newly saved person embraces the new creation and forgives himself.

## THE ADVENTURE OF HOLINESS:

*[15]But be holy in all you do, just as God, the One who called you, is holy. [16]It is written in the Scriptures: "You must be holy, because I am holy."* **1 Peter 1:15-16 (NCV)**

The fundamental idea of holiness is that of separation from the world and sinful defilement. It also implies a consecration and devotion to God.

- When we are holy, we are sharing in the purity of God while we are abstaining from the things of this world which bring defilement and cause us to live a sinful life.
- Holiness means that we examine how well we accept or reject the world's values.
- Please note that holiness does not mean we abstain from life, but that we refrain from sin.
- Living a holy life means that we are devoted to service to God, and that means we can lead active and fully involved lives.
- Belonging to and being fully involved in a church helps you develop holiness because you can focus on helping others as a means of serving the Lord Jesus Christ.
- There is a correlation between holiness and Christian love (agape). The more you can love your brothers and sisters the greater the opportunity for holiness. *[1]Everyone who believes that*

*Jesus is the Christ is God's child, and whoever loves the Father also loves the Father's children.* **1 John 5:1 (NCV**

## THE ADVENTURE OF GODLY SERVICE:

*⁶In the past, the law held us like prisoners, but our old selves died, and we were made free from the law. So now we serve God in a new way with the Spirit, and not in the old way with written rules.* **Romans 7:6 (NCV)**

When in bondage to sin, we could not serve God because we could not have fellowship with him or even hear how he wanted us to serve him.

- Trying to serve him by keeping the law (or church dogma rules and regulations) leads merely to legalism rather than genuine service.
- Christians are to serve with spiritual power. A power received through the Baptism of the Holy Spirit which enables Christians to serve under the guidance and direction of the Holy Spirit.
- Serving with the power of the Holy Spirit was a "new" way for Paul but should be a standard way of operating in the present-day Christian church.
- Since everyone can receive the Holy Spirit, everyone should have some form of service within the body of Christ.
- Not every form of service is the same, but the necessity of serving is universal to us all.
- While we are serving the church, we are attempting to please God, and that is the significant measure of our success. If God tells us to clean out the bathrooms, we do so to please him even though we received no immediate reward and find the task nauseating.

## THE ADVENTURE OF A VICTORIOUS LIFE:

*³Loving God means obeying his commands. And God's commands are not too hard for us, ⁴because everyone who is a child of God conquers the world. And this is the victory that conquers the world—our faith.* **1 John 5:3-4 (NCV)**

We all suffer from many kinds of physical, emotional, and spiritual conditions which are painful and difficult for us to overcome.

- We have a promise from God that if we keep his commandments, we will have victory.
- We can keep his commandments because we are members of his family, and he has given us the power to live the kind of life that is pleasing to him.
- That supernatural and Godly spiritual power can overcome every circumstance, and give us victory regardless of our situation.
- For us to have the victory over the burdens of life, we must believe that Jesus has given it to us since he overcame the world.
- There is a distinct correlation between faith and victory. The more we believe that Christ gave us the victory, the more success we will have in our lives. If we have little faith in the promises of Jesus, then we will have little victory in our lives. Also, the less we trust Jesus then, the less power we will receive to overcome.
- Once we understand that each challenge we face is an opportunity to grow closer to God and to have victory, then we will experience victory after victory throughout life.

## CONCLUSION:

Salvation brings change to who we are and in the way we live. We genuinely begin a series of adventures, a voyage that ends in eternal life with God in heaven but starts with the cross on earth. Our companion is Jesus Christ, our guide is the Holy Spirit, and the one we please is Father God. If we press on in these adventures, nothing can defeat us, and no one or thing can stop us. To God be the glory!

## NOTES:

# Thirty-Eight
## WHERE TO TURN WHEN THE WORLD IS FALLING APART

**T**ext: ¹⁹We *know that we are from God and that the whole world lies under the control of the evil one.* **1 John 5:19 (NCV)**

### INTRODUCTION:

As I write this sermon my heart is heavy with the knowledge that the world is, apparently, falling apart.

- We see an unprecedented increase in Christian persecution not only aboard but within our nation.
- We face a political system that not only disdains our faith but seems to support the enemies of Christ.
- Our nation has been and may be governed by an ideology foreign to our constitution, and those in control seemed to have lost common sense to the point of total moral and ethical confusion.
- We are overwhelmed by the criminal behavior we see on our streets and have lost confidence that those sworn to protect us will do so, and that they may be part of the problem rather than the solution.
- We are experiencing a spike in racism and racial hatred as well as bigotry of all sorts.
- We are dismayed that there are so few Christian voices calling for repentance and restoration of our national unity.

The purpose of this sermon is to determine what the Word has to say about all of this and, by doing so, give us spiritual guidance.

Jerome A. Jochem M.S., M.A.

## WE ARE FROM GOD:

During times such as these, it becomes obvious that there are two opposing kingdoms in the world. One of God consisting of those who are from God, and another dark kingdom consisting of those who do the works and maintain the theology of Satan.

- It is a powerful tactic of the Devil to produce as much confusion about the two kingdoms as possible. Especially, which kingdom is which - which god is God?
- Scripture gives us a simple solution to cut through the confusion: Those who are from the kingdom of God know this because they have the Spirit of God. *[13] We know that we live in him and he in us, because he has given us of his Spirit.* **1 John 4:13 (NIV)**
- We also know the Spirit that we have is that of God because we have accepted Jesus Christ as our Lord and Savior. *[2] This is how you can recognize the Spirit of God: Every spirit that acknowledges that Jesus Christ has come in the flesh is from God.* **1 John 4:2 (NIV)**
- Having made that commitment to Christ, we can confidently say that we belong to God's kingdom and we are from God.
- Scripture also tells us how we can know who belongs to the Devil's kingdom: *[3] but every spirit that does not acknowledge Jesus is not from God. This is the spirit of the antichrist, which you have heard is coming and even now is already in the world.* **1 John 4:3 (NIV)**
- In the midst of all the political lies, religious persecution, and moral confusion, we can tell a lie from the truth because we have the Spirit of God, and we are of God: *[6] We are from God, and whoever knows God listens to us; but whoever is not from God does not listen to us. This is how we recognize the Spirit of truth and the spirit of falsehood.* **1 John 4:6 (NIV)**

## JOHN'S SOLUTION:

The Apostle John's solution to all the confusion and deception that we are dealing with today is straightforward. If you confess that Jesus is your Lord and believe in your heart that God raised him from the dead, then you have the Spirit of God in you, and you are from God.

- Having the Spirit within you means that you can discern the lies of the kingdom of darkness from the truths of the kingdom of God.
- In other words, the Spirit will teach you how to discern using the Word, and you will be able to know what is true and what is false.
- Since you have the Spirit of truth within, you can also tell who is deceived and who is believing in a falsehood.
- Now, John's solution is not politically correct because it demands fidelity to Christ and produces conclusions based on the Word of God.
- Be aware that if you stand on John's solution, you will be persecuted and labeled in the most negative ways.

## WORLD UNDER THE CONTROL OF THE EVIL ONE:

John uses the word "world" as a symbol of wickedness and spiritual corruption. Both wickedness and spiritual corruptions are symptoms or reflections of the spiritual forces that control the world.

- We should not be surprised, then if the world is full of hatred, violence, moral perversion, and destruction because the one who controls it is characterized by the desire to 'kill, steal, and destroy". [16] *These are the ways of the world: wanting to please our sinful selves, wanting the sinful things we see, and being too proud of what we have. None of these come from the Father, but all of them come from the world.* **1 John 2:16 (NCV)**
- There are limitations to this control in that the Evil One can only control those of his kingdom.
- Jesus overcame the world, and through him, we are free of it as well: [4]*because everyone who is a child of God conquers the world. And this is the victory that conquers the world—our faith. [5]So the one who wins against the world is the person who believes that Jesus is the Son of God.* **1 John 5:4-5 (NCV***)*
- We should not be astonished that the world opposes and hates us and attempts to force us to conform to its temptations. After all, the Evil One wants to control us by making us part of his kingdom. Scripture warns us of the rage that follows when we refuse to conform to the world: [19] *if you belonged to the world, it would love you as it loves its own. But I have chosen you out of*

> *the world, so you don't belong to it. That is why the world hates you.* **John 15:19 (NCV)**

- If we make a point of shinning the light of Jesus into the dark world, then we need to be prepared to suffer for his name's sake. Jesus told us to remember that [18] *"If the world hates you, remember that it hated me first.* **John 15:18 (NCV)**

## CONCLUSION:

As the world continues to try to force us to conform to its dictates, we need to remember that we belong to God and his kingdom. Indeed, in his prayer for us, Christ said: [14] *I have given them your teaching. And the world has hated them, because they don't belong to the world, just as I don't belong to the world.* [15] *I am not asking you to take them out of the world but to keep them safe from the Evil One.* [16] *They don't belong to the world, just as I don't belong to the world.* **John 17:14-16 (NCV)**

We are to stand firm. We are to declare our faith, despite the consequences. We are to boldly speak the Word and refuse to conform to that which demeans it. Suffering may be our service, but his kingdom is our reward. [33] *"I told you these things so that you can have peace in me. In this world you will have trouble but be brave! I have defeated the world."* **John 16:33 (NCV)**

## NOTES:

# Thirty-Nine

## THE MISUNDERSTOOD TITHE

**ext:** *⁴²How terrible for you Pharisees! You give God one-tenth of even your mint, your rue, and every other plant in your garden. But you fail to be fair to others and to love God. These are the things you should do while continuing to do those other things.* **Luke 11:42 (NCV)**

### INTRODUCTION:

I believe that many pastors do not track what individual church members give to the Lord each week. They don't monitor personal tithes because they sincerely believe that what you give is between you and God. Many pastors review yearly giving as they prepare the tax forms and find that very few church families are tithing. I wrote this sermon to address the lack of understanding as to why you must tithe if you wish to prosper in the Lord.

### QUALIFIER:

I am not preaching this sermon because of selfish reasons.

- I am not trying to get more money from you because I want a raise or because I want to profit personally.
- I hope you realize that as your pastor, I do tithe and give to the church above the tithe. I can do this not because I make a lot of money, but because I have learned the importance of tithing.
- I admit that if you are not tithing, then I have failed you. I have neglected to teach you the importance of tithing.
- This sermon is not about me; it is about you and your future prosperity.

Jerome A. Jochem M.S., M.A.

## A QUICK REVIEW:

There is a lot of reading materials available that justify the tithe in the New Testament church, but I want to make a few points that are relevant to the tithe today:

- The tithe was established in the Old Testament when Abraham gave 10% to Melchisedec King of Salem and who was an Old Testament figure of Christ. (Genesis 14:18-20)
- Throughout the rest of the Old Testament, the nature of the tithe was refined to be the first fruits brought to the local storehouse.
- It is extremely important to realize that the tithe is to be given to the church and not to other ministries no matter how important or fruitful: *⁴Don't worship the LORD your God that way, ⁵but look for the place the LORD your God will choose—a place among your tribes where he is to be worshiped. Go there, ⁶and bring to that place your burnt offerings and sacrifices; bring a tenth of what you gain and your special gifts; bring what you have promised and the special gifts you want to give the LORD, and bring the first animals born to your herds and flocks.* **Deuteronomy 12:4-6 (NCV)**
- The tithe is God's money, not yours and to not tithe is literally to steal from God.

  *⁸"Should a person rob God? But you are robbing me. "You ask, 'How have we robbed you?' "You have robbed me in your offerings and the tenth of your crops. ⁹So a curse is on you, because the whole nation has robbed me. ¹⁰Bring to the storehouse a full tenth of what you earn so there will be food in my house. Test me in this," says the LORD All-Powerful. "I will open the windows of heaven for you and pour out all the blessings you need ¹¹I will stop the insects so they won't eat your crops. The grapes won't fall from your vines before they are ready to pick," says the LORD All-Powerful. ¹²"All the nations will call you blessed, because you will have a pleasant country," says the LORD All-Powerful.* **Malachi 3:8-12 (NCV)**

## DYNAMICS OF THE TITHE:

Like everything that God asks of us, the tithe is dynamic and produces blessings. The tithe also carries with it a warning of a curse which can cause us deep trouble if we are not careful. Let us look at the curse first and then follow up with the blessings of meeting the tithe.

## THE CURSE:

Robbing God of his tithe produces a curse on your life that takes the shape of poverty, sickness, broken relationships, and failed futures.

- If you are a Christian and you are not tithing, then you are dishonoring God and stealing from him for your personal use. You are saved, and your sins are forgiven, but the future that God wants for you will not take place because you are putting money above God. God is not in second place and less important than your bills or debts.

- Stealing from God will open the door to Satan, and Satan will get your tithe. He will steal it from you through doctor bills, repairs to your car or house, loss of jobs, and such unforeseen things as accidents,

- Satan will take even more from you than your tithe money. Add up your expenses for medical services or car repairs and see if it isn't much greater than your tithe.

- The next time you decide not to tithe, or you tell yourself that you don't have enough money to tithe, ask yourself if you want to remain poor, sick, or defeated. If the answer to that question is no, then tithe.

- If you believe that God is calling you to a ministry of some sort, and you are not tithing, then ask yourself if God can trust you with the spiritual well-being of others when you are stealing from him something as mundane as money? Can you efficiently minister while you are dishonoring God or are you just being a hypocrite?

- If a minister wants his ministry to be blessed then one of the first things he needs to do is learn to tithe and make it a rule, even a habit in his life.

- Not tithing can have serious spiritual consequences for the lost. A church that does not have the means to minister the Gospel will not see the lost saved, and those refusing to tithe bear the responsibility and consequences of that loss.

The characteristics of someone under the curse of not tithing are prevalent as listed below:

- He has more debts than he can handle. He is a slave to debt
- He cannot make ends meet. When he gets a bit ahead of the game, something happens to knock him off his feet.
- He is always under financial stress and worries about how he can pay his bills.
- He is hit continuously by unexpected attacks on his pocketbook.
- He does not have the resources to deal with his or his family's needs.
- He has no financial peace.

## The Blessings:

When you tithe, you are blessed by God because you are honoring him and by giving him the first fruits of your labor. Remember though that the tithe belongs to the Lord and it is his because he provides it for you to give.

- Giving your tithe becomes a form of worship and praise. So, when you tithe to the church, you are worshiping him and thanking him for what he has given to you.
- When you tithe you are demonstrating your trust in God and that he is your resource and will pour out all the blessings you need. He will see to it that you can pay your bills even if you have no idea where the money is coming from, even out of the *"windows of heaven."* (Vs. 10)
- Tithing is like using fertilizer in that if you fertilize your fields you will harvest a more significant crop.
- By tithing, you enable God to prevent Satan's major attacks in either their intensity or frequency.
- While Satan may still attack, even in some dramatically expensive ways, God will nullify the attack by providing the way out. You will be able to pay the bills to get treatment for the disease, repair the broken parts, or recover from the accident. All of this is more reason to praise him.
- By tithing, God will set you free from debt and bill collectors.
- By tithing, you show your respect for God, and he will cause your ministry to flourish.

## CHARACTERISTICS OF A TITHER:

- He lives in financial peace.
- When he has an expense beyond his means, he is confident that God will provide.
- He is sure that when Satan attacks, God counters the attack by his provision.
- He makes a conscious attempt to set aside money to tithe. Tithing has become a habit.
- He rebukes the temptation not to tithe and will tithe at a sacrifice to what he may owe the world.
- He goes beyond just his tithe and gives offerings and his time and labor to the Lord.

## CONCLUSION:

Ask yourself what kind of church do you want? Do you want a church that is struggling to pay its bills, or cannot minister the Gospel because it does not have the means to do so? Do you want a church building that is run down and not taken care of because it can't afford to make the repairs and changes needed to be honored as God's house of worship? Do you want a church that cannot help other people because it's not following God's command to provide for itself? Continue to tithe if your answer to these questions is no. If your answer to these questions is yes, then do not tithe. When you start to tithe, you might have to start small, but you will be delighted and amazed at how quickly God will pour out blessings on you and your family. Above all else, do not misunderstand the tithe, it is not a suggestion, it is a command!

## NOTES:

# *Forty*

# CHRIST OUR VALENTINE

**T**ext: ¹*You are God's children whom he loves, so try to be like him.* ²*Live a life of love just as Christ loved us and gave himself for us as a sweet-smelling offering and sacrifice to God.* **Ephesians 5:1-2 (NCV)**

⁹*I loved you as the Father loved me. Now remain in my love.* ¹⁰*I have obeyed my Father's commands, and I remain in his love. In the same way, if you obey my commands, you will remain in my love.* **John 15:9-10 (NCV)**

## INTRODUCTION:
Valentine's Day is a time in which we try to express our love for others by giving special gifts or tokens of our love. For those who believe, our most fabulous Valentine is Christ. In this sermon, I would like to examine some of the ways that Christ expressed his love as our special valentine.

## LOVE FOR HIS FATHER:
³⁰*I will not talk with you much longer, because the ruler of this world is coming. He has no power over me,* ³¹*but the world must know that I love the Father, so I do exactly what the Father told me to do. "Come now, let us go.* **John 14:30-31 (NCV)**

- Jesus expressed his love for the Father by his obedience even unto death.
- Because of his great love for his Father, he was willing and even eager to express that love so that the world would recognize that he loves the Father and that the Father loves him.

- Please note that he did not give Satan any credit for what was about to happen to him, but instead, he identified his sacrifice as a love offering in obedience to his Father's will.

## LOVE FOR HIS CHURCH:

*[9] I loved you as the Father loved me. Now remain in my love. [10] I have obeyed my Father's commands, and I remain in his love. In the same way, if you obey my commands, you will remain in my love. [11] I have told you these things so that you can have the same joy I have and so that your joy will be the fullest possible joy.* **John 15:9-11 (NCV)**

- In his sacrificial death, Jesus was obedient to the command and will of his Father. It is clear in this Scripture that he feels we also should be obedient to his commandments to remain in his love.
- Remember that his commandments consist of two directives. The first is to love God and the second is to love each other.
- To abide or remain in his love, we must love God and each other. If we do this, then he promises that we will continue in his love which makes it possible to love others even more deeply.
- In other words, to live a life of love we must first love God and then each other, and in doing so, our lives are based on love which becomes dominant in our lifestyle.

## LOVE FOR THOSE WHO LOVE HIM:

*[21] Those who know my commands and obey them are the ones who love me, and my Father will love those who love me. I will love them and will show myself to them.* **John 14:21 (NCV)**

- Once again, we see the importance of knowing and keeping Christ's commandment to love God and each other.
- Note how love flows in that by loving Christ, his Father loves us and he will show his love for us.
- The Scripture includes the promise that those who love Christ by keeping his commandments will have a continuous revelation of that love that is progressive and experiential.

## LOVE FOR THE LOST:

*[10] The Son of Man came to find lost people and save them.* **Luke 19:10 (NCV)**

- There is no stronger demonstration of Christ's love than that of his intense desire to save the lost.
- What is radical about the Scripture is that he came to save those who reject his love rather than those who accept his love.
- Note also that in the Scripture, this active seeking of those who need him is still true today as an expression of his love for them.

## 4 TYPES OF LOVE OF CHRIST
1. Self-sacrificing.
2. Interceding love.
3. Providing.
4. Eternal.

1). Self-sacrifice: [16] *This is how we know what real love is: Jesus gave his life for us. So we should give our lives for our brothers and sisters.* **1 John 3:16 (NCV)**
- As Christ's love was sacrificial, we may also be expected to sacrifice for our brothers and sisters.
- While our lives may not be due as a sacrifice, most often we are expected to care for, provide for, and aid our brothers and sisters in practical ways as an expression of our love for them.
- We must each actively search for the small sacrifices we can make to love our brothers and sisters as a way of honoring the real love that Jesus had for us.

2). Interceding: [25] *So he is able always to save those who come to God through him, because he always lives, asking God to help them.* **Hebrews 7:25 (NCV)**
- Christ loves us by interceding for us. This occurs in the present because Christ is alive today.
- It is amazing to think that we have a high priest who knows us individually and who is willing to intercede for us even in some cases with the smallest requests for a blessing.

3). Providing: [7]*But I tell you the truth, it is better for you that I go away. When I go away, I will send the Helper to you. If I do not go away, the Helper will not come.* **John 16:7 (NCV)**
- Love never abandons those who are truly loved.

- In this Scripture, Jesus was simply saying that he would not be with the apostles or with us physically but would send the Holy Spirit to be with us when he was with his Father in heaven.
- As Christ loves us so does the Spirit. Thus, the love of God continues throughout history. God's provision of his love is continuous throughout time.

4). Eternal: [38] *Yes, I am sure that neither death, nor life, nor angels, nor ruling spirits, nothing now, nothing in the future, no powers,* [39] *nothing above us, nothing below us, nor anything else in the whole world will ever be able to separate us from the love of God that is in Christ Jesus our Lord.* **Romans 8:38-39 (NCV)**

- This Scripture reassures us that God's love is with us even during troubled times.
- Jesus not only told us that we would have trouble times, but he promised that he would be with us and that he has already overcome those troubles.
- Because of the love of Jesus in our lives, we can become overcomers and be victorious in life. This victory is due to the eternal love of God for us who believe.

## CONCLUSION:

God gave us an excellent and precious valentine; whose name is Jesus Christ. He is the direct expression of God's love for us, and he is the way that we can come to a deep and profound love of God. There couldn't be a better Valentine than the one who gives us eternal life and eternal relationship with the God who is love.

## NOTES:

# *Forty-One*

# HOLY COMMUNION

**T**ext: *²³The teaching I gave you is the same teaching I received from the Lord: On the night when the Lord Jesus was handed over to be killed, he took bread ²⁴and gave thanks for it. Then he broke the bread and said, "This is my body; it is for you. Do this to remember me." ²⁵In the same way, after they ate, Jesus took the cup. He said, "This cup is the new agreement that is sealed with the blood of my death. When you drink this, do it to remember me." ²⁶Every time you eat this bread and drink this cup you are telling others about the Lord's death until he comes.* **1 Corinthians 11:23-26 (NCV)**

## INTRODUCTION:

The celebration of Holy Communion is an ordinance of the church. We do it because we are commanded to celebrate communion by the Lord as a memorial to him. We cannot reduce Holy Communion to the status of a ritual, mindlessly repeated like we are robots on an assembly line. Holy Communion is derived from the Passover meal. Jesus modified the Seder so that we can rejoice at our freedom from slavery to sin that he purchased for us on the cross. In this sermon, I intend to preach about some of the beautiful aspects of Holy Communion which we should never forget.

## THE BREAD:

Jesus said that he was the bread that came down from heaven and was also the bread of life. (John 6:35) Jesus knew that the most significant physical gift that God gave us was the body.

- Without our bodies, we can do nothing in this world.

- God incarnated in a body at the birth of Christ to directly impact the world. His body was a vehicle for divinity
- When he was crucified, he offered his body as a sacrifice. A substitute for us as the sacrificial lamb.
- During the Passover meal, the bread is unleavened. Leaven represents sin. Jesus who was without sin offered his body which like the bread of Passover, was broken for us.
- The sacrifice of the Lamb of God was complete and involved the death of his body as a substitute for our spiritual and physical death due to sin.

## THE BLOOD:

*[11]This is because the life of the body is in the blood, and I have given you rules for pouring that blood on the altar to remove your sins so you will belong to the LORD. It is the blood that removes the sins, because it is life.*
**Leviticus 17:11 (NCV)**

- Jesus said that his blood established the New Covenant between God and humanity. The New Covenant is possible because his blood removes the sin of a believer.
- Since blood represents the life of a person, the blood of Christ represents his life.
- In other words, the forgiveness of our sins is possible because Jesus gave his life for our sake.
- The altar was the cross; the blood was from his body; the forgiveness of our sins was from his love.

## THE MEANING OF COMMUNION:

Jesus told us that we must eat his body and drink his blood. (John 6:53-55)

- The Roman Catholic Church takes this literally. They believe that a transformation takes place in the bread and wine of communion and that both become the literal body and blood of Christ.
- Evangelical Christians do not believe that Christ was speaking literally, but that he was talking symbolically.
- To eat his body and drink his blood means that we must assimilate Christ.
- To assimilate Jesus means that we must bring into our walk with him, his character, his love, and his willingness to sacrifice.

Jerome A. Jochem M.S., M.A.

## CONCLUSION:

As we celebrate Holy Communion, let us remember that he sacrificed everything for us. Jesus held nothing back so that our sins were forgiven, and we can become the children of God. We should also remember that he will return to us, and as we partake in communion, we are affirming his promise of eternal life.

## NOTES:

# TWO MIRACLES OF CHRISTMAS

**T**ext: *³⁴Mary said to the angel, "How will this happen since I am a virgin?" ³⁵The angel said to Mary, "The Holy Spirit will come upon you, and the power of the Most High will cover you. For this reason the baby will be holy and will be called the Son of God.* **Luke 1:34-35 (NCV)**

## INTRODUCTION:
While we tend to focus on the celebratory aspect of Christmas, Christmas contains two profound mysteries based on two equally profound miracles. These mysteries and wonders provide a richness to Christianity unparalleled in any other religion because they are supernatural.

## THE ORDER OF MIRACLES:
Both the Old and New Testaments are full of miracles and works of wonder. The ultimate purpose is to demonstrate the nature of God and confirm his sovereignty over the universe of things and men. Miracles are of three general types:

1. Type 1 is a supernatural control of natural events in intensity, duration, or sequence.
2. Type 2 is a supernatural modification or suspension of the laws that govern the universe.
3. Type 3 is a supernatural miracle that is a combination of types 1 and 2.

In the story of Christmas, we can see at least two distinct types of miracles in operation.

Jerome A. Jochem M.S., M.A.

## HIS CONCEPTION:
[34]*Mary said to the angel, "How will this happen since I am a virgin?"* (Vs. 34)

The Old Testament word "virgin" can mean a young woman. (Isaiah 7:14, Genesis. 24:43)
- It is evident that Mary was talking about the usual way of becoming pregnant.
- In human conception, there usually must be a Y chromosome contributed by a male. In the virgin birth, there was no male to contribute the Y chromosome.
- While a woman can clone a woman (XX), she cannot clone a male (XY) because the Y chromosome is missing.

The conception of Jesus was, a type 2 miracle because God bypassed the standard rules of human conception.

## MARVELS OF POWER:
So, the question is how Mary could give birth to a baby boy without the ordinary means of conception in play?

*"The Holy Spirit will come upon you, and the power of the Most High will cover you."* (Vs. 35a)
- The type 2 miracle, in this case, had to do with the modification of the laws of genetics.
- The power of the Holy Spirit must have either converted an X chromosome into a Y chromosome or created a Y chromosome supernaturally. So, Jesus was born a male.

## HIS IDENTITY:
*…For this reason the baby will be holy and will be called the Son of God.* (Vs. 35b)

While the mechanism of the virgin birth was miraculous, the virgin birth has more significance regarding the identity of Jesus.
- Since no husband was involved in his birth, the fact is that God the Father was indeed the father of Jesus through the power of the Holy Spirit.
- Jesus can be legitimately called the only begotten Son of God.

His identity is a type three miracle because of the virgin birth, but also because Jesus through born as a human is also God. What is a natural event (birth) was now a supernatural event never seen in history and will never occur again!

- He is fully human with all the characteristics of humanity, but without a sin nature.
- He is entirely God capable of all the manifestations of the divine, but with self-imposed limitations on his divinity.

In his conception, we see both the natural order of the universe changed, and the rules of genetics modified so the savior can be born as both God and man.

## CONCLUSION:

This Christmas remember the two great miracles and mysteries that we celebrate at the birth of our Lord Jesus Christ. His birth was a supernatural miracle, and his personhood was equally a remarkable combination of divinity and humanity. Since Christianity is all about Jesus, you can see that it is indeed one of the most supernatural religions in the world.

## NOTES:

# *Forty-Three*

# CHRISTMAS -THE PREEXISTENT SON

**T**ext: *²⁶ During Elizabeth's sixth month of pregnancy, God sent the angel Gabriel to Nazareth, a town in Galilee, ²⁷ to a virgin. She was engaged to marry a man named Joseph from the family of David. Her name was Mary. ²⁸ The angel came to her and said, "Greetings! The Lord has blessed you and is with you. " ²⁹ But Mary was very startled by what the angel said and wondered what this greeting might mean. ³⁰ The angel said to her, "Don't be afraid, Mary; God has shown you his grace. ³¹ Listen! You will become pregnant and give birth to a son, and you will name him Jesus. ³² He will be great and will be called the Son of the Most High. The Lord God will give him the throne of King David, his ancestor. ³³ He will rule over the people of Jacob forever, and his kingdom will never end. " ³⁴ Mary said to the angel, "How will this happen since I am a virgin? " ³⁵ The angel said to Mary, "The Holy Spirit will come upon you, and the power of the Most High will cover you. For this reason the baby will be holy and will be called the Son of God.* **Luke 1:26-35 (NCV)**

## INTRODUCTION:

Our text for today tells us that Jesus is called the Son of God because the Holy Spirit conceived him. Admittedly, it is difficult to understand who was conceived by the Holy Spirit, even though the angel said that he would be the son of God. The question that we must ask ourselves this Christmas is who was conceived, who became Jesus Christ, and who is this son of the most high God? To answer these questions, we must keep two specific facts in mind:

## THE DIVINE WORD:

*¹ In the beginning there was the Word. The Word was with God, and the Word was God. ² He was with God in the beginning. ³ All things were made by him, and nothing was made without him· ⁴ In him there was life, and that life was the light of all people.* **John 1:1-4 (NCV)**

The Greek meaning of "Word" is "Logos" which means something said (including a thought); by implication a topic. It can also imply mental reasoning or especially the Divine Expression.

- In the beginning, before anything was made, God had his best idea ever. To send his son who was with him and who was the savior the world needed.
- His son was his expression of himself, and so his Son is God.
- Since God is a person, his son was also the person who was with God in the beginning.
- Through this person, who was God, all things were made, but he was not made but always had been.
- It was that person who incarnated into human form.
- The incarnation did not make him the son because he already was the son of the Most High God. This means that the son pre-existed before he became Jesus.

## THE IMPORTANCE OF HIS PREEXISTENCE:

If the son had not existed before his incarnation as Jesus, then there would be profound consequences.

- If Christ came into existence at his birth, then no eternal Trinity exists.
- If Christ was not preexistent, then he could not be God, because according to his basic nature, God is eternal.
- Since Christ claimed to be pre-existent, and if he was not pre-existent, then he was a deceiver and a liar. We would have to ask ourselves what else did he lie about or how else did he deceive us? Our very salvation is brought into doubt.

## THE EVIDENCE:

- In the Book of John, Jesus declared that he came down from heaven. This divine origin attests to preexistence before birth. (John 3:13)

- Our text states that Jesus as the son of God was involved in creating the universe. This means that he had to exist before anything else was created. He was in existence before our universe.
- The son was with God before he became Jesus. Later he claimed equality of nature with God (John 10:30). Since he was with God from before the beginning, he claimed equal glory with the Father before the world began.
- Because he was God as the Word or self-expression of God, he claimed full deity and others agreed with his claim. (Colossians 2:9). His attributes as God prove his pre-existence.

## CONCLUSION:

We celebrate the birth of Jesus Christ at Christmas. We are also celebrating the coming into human form of the pre-existent Son of the Most High God. It was God, expressing himself through the son who was born in that manger so many years ago. It was God, entering our world to eventually bring us back to him through Christ his only begotten son. Christmas is the celebration of the love of God for us, such a great love that he sent us his only begotten son. What a magnificent Christmas gift.

## NOTES:

# THE RESURRECTION BODY

**T**ext: *²⁰But Christ has truly been raised from the dead—the first one and proof that those who sleep in death will also be raised.* **1 Corinthians 15:20 (NCV)**

*²⁵Jesus said to her, "I am the resurrection and the life. Those who believe in me will have life even if they die.* **John 11:25 (NCV)**

## INTRODUCTION:

After Christ was crucified and buried, Scriptures unquestionably state that he experienced something never seen before, he resurrected from the dead. We celebrate this event every Easter Sunday, but do we understand what such a resurrection means to us? In this sermon, I intend to discuss several options we have to understand the resurrection, both Christ's and ours. I shall do this by discussing some of the concepts that compete with the doctrine of the resurrection.

## NOT JUST RAISED:

The Scriptures describe cases in which dead people were brought back to life, the case of Lazarus being the most notable. Often the word "raised" is used interchangeably with the word "resurrection," but there are distinct differences between the two concepts:

- To be raised means that the person returned from the dead in the same body which died.
- Being raised means that a total body healing took place and the person was once more alive. (John 11:43 - 44)
- Being raised does not imply immortality. Raised people were to die again as time passes.

Jerome A. Jochem M.S., M.A.

- Being resurrected means that the person returns from the dead in a new body that will not die again. (Romans 6:9)
- The new resurrection body appears to be like the old body that died, but it has different abilities and capacities.
- The resurrection body is immortal and interacts with the universe differently.

So, the resurrection body is a raised body with new attributes and powers that are dramatically more powerful than a raised body.

## NOT A GHOST:

*36 While the two followers were telling this, Jesus himself stood right in the middle of them and said, "Peace be with you." 37 They were fearful and terrified and thought they were seeing a ghost.*

*38 But Jesus said, "Why are you troubled? Why do you doubt what you see? 39 Look at my hands and my feet. It is I myself! Touch me and see, because a ghost does not have a living body as you see I have."* **Luke 24:36-39 (NCV)**

When Jesus appeared to his disciples, they experienced fear and thought that he was a ghost.

- Part of the reason they thought he was a ghost is that he appeared right before them and they did not see him come from anywhere in the room. His sudden and unexpected appearance was what they considered a spirit or ghost would do.
- Jesus understood their confusion and pointed to the fact that his body was solid, touchable, real, alive, and no longer dead.
- Our resurrection is not just mystical but involves a physical body similar in appearance to the bodies we had before death and resurrection took place.
- Jesus will return to us, not as a spirit or ghost, but in his resurrected body.

As a side issue, please note that Jesus did not rebuke his disciples for believing in ghosts. He seems to confirm that ghosts do exist and that they do not have physical bodies.

## NOT REINCARNATION:

Reincarnation is an Asian concept in which a person is reborn into a new life form after death. The life form is determined by karma, which in turn is based on the amount of good or evil done during the person's life.

- Christians have confused resurrection with reincarnation because they do not understand the difference between being resurrected only once and being repeatedly reincarnated.
- While the soul of the reincarnated person can have a body of an animal or insect, the resurrected body always remains human and never takes the form of any other species.
- Scripture refutes reincarnation explicitly because it tells us: *27Just as everyone must die once and be judged*, **Hebrews 9:27 (NCV)**
- Biblically, the doctrine of reincarnation is considered to be heresy or false doctrine.

## NOT NIRVANA:

Nirvana is another Asian concept which is similar to enlightenment; Nirvana refers to a psychological state of detachment from the world and union with the universe.

- Nirvana is achieved through meditation and years of practice. It has nothing to do with resurrection because there is no promise of an afterlife in the sense that most westerners understand it.
- The closest analogy is that nirvana is a state wherein the individual is absorbed into the universe, losing their identity and individual consciousness.
- None of these concepts apply to resurrection.
- While it is desirable to recognize our union with Christ, such a union does not involve the loss of self-identity or submergence of our personality.

## NOT TRANSLATION:

In the Old Testament, Enoch, and Elijah were taken up to heaven by God. This transference from earth to heaven took place without the intervention of death.

Translation is an Old Testament concept that does not apply to resurrection because:

- Christ died.
- Christ was not brought to earth by the resurrection but went from the place of the dead to earth.

## NOT A VISION:

Was the resurrected Christ real or just a vision? Was the resurrected Christ the product of grieving minds or induced hallucinations? Scripture tells us otherwise:

- Any kind of vision is purely mental, but Christ's body was real, touchable, and could eat food.
- Visions tend to be individual events not shared by large groups unless chemically induced.
- A large number of people (500) saw the resurrected Christ, while his apostles touched his wounds and ate with him.
- Even chemically induced visions tend to be unique to the person, and while a number of people may have chemically induced visions, the visions or hallucinations differ from person to person.

## NOT A MYTH OR ALLEGORY:

Myths are symbolic representations of gods. The world is full of mythical gods of the sky, harvest, and food. Allegories are symbolic stories or fables told to prove a point or communicate a principle.

- The resurrection of Jesus is specific to a defined time and place and is testified to by actual people who became determined to tell their experiences to the world.
- The resurrection is not a symbol of an event or an allegory. It is a concrete event that has historical support.
- After several thousand years, we are still relating to the resurrected Jesus through the Holy Spirit, wherein myths fade away and become cultural folktales as superstition is replaced by fact.

## CONCLUSION:

The resurrection of Christ holds a great promise for us and should be celebrated with joy and amazement. As he was the first fruits, we are to follow him with our resurrected bodies. Just as his body had new abilities and capabilities, so will ours. Just as his loved ones recognized his resurrected body, so will ours. Just as his resurrected body had new tasks and works to perform for his Father, so will ours.

## NOTES:

# Forty - Five

# THE EASTER POWER OF HIS DEATH

**T**ext: *²Let us look only to Jesus, the One who began our faith and who makes it perfect. He suffered death on the cross. But he accepted the shame as if it were nothing because of the joy that God put before him. And now he is sitting at the right side of God's throne.* **Hebrews 12:2 (NCV)**

## INTRODUCTION:

Today's sermon concerns the death of Jesus Christ. I am not going to become elaborate theologically, but I'm going to focus on what is basic for you to know because without knowing the basic facts of either the crucifixion or the resurrection you are theologically lost.

## THE DEATH OF JESUS CHRIST:

The central focus of the death of Christ consists of some fundamental ideas. In fact, there are four such essential doctrines.

1. Christ's death was a substitution for sinners.
2. Christ's death was redemption from sin.
3. Christ's death was a reconciliation in God's relationship to man.
4. Christ's death was a propitiation offered to God.

We can call the death of Christ a significant manifestation of God's love. We can see it as an example for us of self-sacrificing, and we would be biblically accurate in making these claims. (John, 15:13; Romans 5:8). But if his death was only a matter of self-sacrifice and love, then we miss the primary importance and meaning of Christ's death.

## SUBSTITUTION:

Of the four primary concepts, we will discuss, substitution is the most powerful and most personal of all. There are two different meanings for substitution:

*⁴He must put his hand on the animal's head, and the LORD will accept it to remove the person's sin so he will belong to God.* **Leviticus 1:4 (NCV)**

In the first case, substitution means that sin is transferred to a sacrifice and the individual sinner becomes reconciled with God. Our sin is transferred to Christ, the Lamb of God, and we became reconciled to God.

*¹⁵"Make the Levites pure, and present them as an offering so that they may come to work at the Meeting Tent. ¹⁶They will be given completely to me from the Israelites; I have taken them for myself instead of the firstborn of every Israelite woman. ¹⁷All the firstborn in Israel—people or animals—are mine. When I killed all the firstborn in Egypt, I set the firstborn in Israel aside for myself. ¹⁸But I have taken the Levites instead of all the firstborn in Israel. ¹⁹From all the Israelites I have given the Levites to Aaron and his sons so that they may serve the Israelites at the Meeting Tent. They will help remove the Israelites' sins so they will belong to the LORD and so that no disaster will strike the Israelites when they approach the Holy Place."* **Numbers 8:15-19 (NCV)**

The second case is found in the above Scripture:

- In this Scripture, the Levites are substituted for the firstborn in Israel. The Levites paid the indebtedness of the firstborn.
- In the same manner, our indebtedness to God is paid for by Jesus

## REDEMPTION:

*¹⁵The king of Egypt was stubborn and refused to let us leave. But the LORD killed every firstborn male in Egypt, both human and animal. That is why I sacrifice every firstborn male animal to the LORD, and that is why I buy back each of my firstborn sons from the LORD.'* **(Exodus 13:15)**

This Scripture implies that redemption is the purchasing back of something that is in debt and always includes a ransom or the payment of a ransom.

- The word redemption has been used nine times in Scripture always accompanied by the idea of a ransom or a price paid.
- The idea running through all the words used for ransom is that Christ's death is a payment that resulted in our being bought back or redeem.
- The debt that we owe God because of our sin is more than canceled. It is paid for entirely by his death.

This means that Christ saves us, not by power, not by belief or doctrine, not by his example, not by his love and finally, not by his moral influence but because he paid the ransom with his death.

In one sense, his death satisfied divine justice, and we are ransomed from the curse and authority of the law and the power of sin.

## RECONCILIATION:

To reconcile ourselves means that we experience a change from antagonism to friendship. It is a mutual change agreed upon by both parties who have had hostility between them.

- In the Book of Colossians, the word reconciliation is used to refer to a change in the personal character of the sinner for he has ceased to be an enemy of God. For example, the Apostle Paul in 2 Corinthians beseeches the Corinthians to be "reconciled to God." That is to lay aside their hostility and anger at God.
- In Romans 5, Paul refers not to ourselves, but to God as the party reconciled. We have received reconciliation from God, that is, he has made us his friends.
- You also will find in 2 Corinthians the same basic idea that God's reconciliation originated with himself and consisted of the removal of his anger and the application of grace in our lives.
- The sins that we all commit justifies and demands punishment. The death of Christ satisfies justice and so reconciles God to us, in other words, God becomes our friend instead of our enemy.

## PROPITIATION:

By far, propitiation is one of the most challenging concepts to conceive of by Christians, because our understanding of propitiation involves two different Greek words. The first meaning can be found in the book of Romans.

- In Romans 3:25 and Hebrews 9:5, which talks about the "mercy seat," the Greek word "Hilasterion" is used.
- This Greek word means "covering," and it refers to the lid of the Ark of the Covenant.
- This word came to mean not only to the mercy seat or lid of the ark but also propitiation by blood.
- Once a year the high priest offered a sacrifice for all the people of Israel. He went behind the veil into the holy place and sprinkled the Ark of the Covenant with blood. He sprinkled the mercy seat with blood and so made propitiation for the people of Israel.
- In like manner, the blood of Christ, which he shed at his death becomes our propitiation and is sprinkled on the mercy seat of the heavenly temple.
- The blood of Christ allows God's forgiveness and pardon for the sinner to become consistent with God's character.
- Christ's propitiation does not cause God to love us or make him more loving; it only makes it consistent for him to exercise his love towards us.

*²He is the way our sins are taken away, and not only our sins but the sins of all people. 1 John 2:2 (NCV)*

In this verse, a different Greek word is used for propitiation. This word is closely associated with the fact that Christ became our substitute and that he took upon himself our sin and paid the price by the punishment he endured. In other words, he paid the price to resolve our guilt and to make propitiation in the sense that we are reconciled to God.

## CONCLUSION:

The willingness of Christ to sacrifice for our sake is impressive. It is an amazing form or demonstration of God's love for us, it is an amazing demonstration of God's willingness to sacrifice himself for us, and it is an amazing and touching personal outreach to each of us, a persuasion to confess our sins, and believe in him. But without a doubt, all these wonderful and surprising aspects of his death are meaningless unless we understand the nature of his substitution, propitiation, and reconciliation and the part they played in our redemption. Once these basic elements are understood, it is easy to claim him as Lord and Savior.

NOTES:

# *Forty-Six*

# INDEPENDENCE DAY

**T**ext: [12] *Happy is the nation whose God is the LORD, the people he chose for his very own.* **Psalms 33:12 (NCV)**

## INTRODUCTION:

Today's Scripture is short but filled with significant meaning and hope for the nation who has God as Lord. Used in the context of this Scripture, Lord can mean "the eternal Ruler and Judge." Our country is founded on three pillars. One of those pillars is the Christian faith. I don't think that anyone who knows history would debate with me about the faith of our founders, a faith expressed in our constitution and which emphasizes freedom. After all, the Declaration of Independence is an expression of faith in God, as our nation became free of the rule of England and free to be an independent self-governing nation. In this sermon, I would like to look at the various kinds of countries that exist in today's world, in relationship to God, and perhaps illustrate some of the dangers that America faces today.

## THE GODLESS NATION:

- Consists of such giant nations as Russia and China, but also includes smaller nations like North Korea. The error of Godlessness does not depend on the size of the country or the number of people in that country.
- The government is based on the idea that God is not needed and any theology or belief in God is evil and against the state's best interest. So, you have the communist doctrine that religion is the "opiate" of the people.

- In these nations, there is no freedom of religion and anyone practicing religion is likely to be persecuted, sometimes in extreme ways.
- While these nations may seem to prosper, their people live in spiritual darkness that grows darker each year. They may be wealthy materially, but they are poverty-struck spiritually.

## THE NATION OF MANY GODS:

- These nations tend to have many gods, some of which are mythical while others are materialistic.
- A good example is India, where there are some 330 gods and goddesses.
- These nations incorporate Jesus as just another god and refuse to see that he is the only real God and Lord.
- As a result, these nations miss the blessings of God, and in extreme cases are overcome by a lack of appreciation for human life and for life itself. Their religion is more superstition rather than truth, and they are culturally bound to keep those superstitions rather than acknowledging Christ.
- Ironically, you would think that these nations have religious tolerance, but the opposite is true. One religion will persecute another, even among the native religions.
- So, there is limited freedom of religion, and much intolerance, especially for Christianity.

## THE NATION WHOSE GOD IS FALSE:

When one thinks of false religion, Islam comes to mind because of the doctrines of Islam that are allegedly from God but prescribe terror, torture, and death for non-believers.

But even our nation has its share of false gods! They are usually expressed as some form of materialism. For example:

- There is a god of money, and Scripture tells us that we cannot worship money and the true God.
- There is a god of power, especially political power. The worship of this god results in corruption.
- There is a god of pleasure, usually including the worship of sex that results in gross immorality.

- There is a god of fame. This god offers the person the idea that a famous person is a special person exempt from the rule of God.

If a nation has so many materialistic gods, it becomes tough to acknowledge the true God, especially if that acknowledgment means giving up a material god.

## THE NATION WHOSE GOD IS THE LORD:

The promise in today's Scripture is meant for Israel. That promise can hold true for any nation that has the genuine God as Lord. The Scripture also contains a promise of a blessing for those who remain true to God. That blessing manifests itself in many ways, for example:

- These nations honor God's dominion. They do not try to substitute human knowledge and wisdom for God.
- These nations acknowledge the power and the right of God to judge the nation. In other words, these nation's function under the rule of God's law.
- These nations respect God in the establishment of their policies towards others. These nations have true freedom of religion given the basic idea that people will find the truth if they can search for it. Christ is available for all those who seek him if the government does not quench their ability to seek him.

## CONCLUSION:

In our nation, there are forces at work to destroy the pillar of the Christian faith as a basis for our national identity. These forces have caused much turmoil and disruption in our nation. We must hold true to the faith in God through Jesus Christ that we have because in that faith we can have peace, prosperity, and a hopeful future. Forces from outside our country are also causing disruption and anarchy. Once again, we see this coming from a religion that is false and destructive. However, this is just another reason why we need to maintain and strengthen our freedom of religion, but also individually participate in worshiping the true God because he is stronger than the enemies who would destroy us.

## NOTES:

# Forty-Seven
## FATHER GOD

**T**ext: *"This, then, is how you should pray:" 'Our Father in heaven,"*
**Matthew 6:9 (NIV)**

### INTRODUCTION:
Jesus often mentioned his Father who is God. Until the time of the New Testament, the character and person of Father God remained a mystery. Jesus came to reveal Father God, and in doing so, we can see the relationship of Jesus to his Father, and the Father's relationship with Jesus. In this sermon, I want to explore the character of Father God, the relationship between Jesus and his Father, and how we can learn from and become better human fathers.

### BIBLICAL FACTS ABOUT FATHER GOD:
Both the New and Old Testaments mention Father God. He is referred to as Father on 271 occasions in the Scriptures.
- 13 times in the Old Testament.
- 258 times in the New Testament.
- 178 times in the Gospels.
- 80 times from Acts through Revelation.

He is mentioned by the title "Father" in six Old Testament books (2 Samuel, 1 Chronicles, Psalms, Isaiah, Jeremiah, Malachi) and every New Testament book, with the single exception of 3 John.

The Old Testament first and final references:
- First reference: 2 Samuel 7:14.
- Final reference: Malachi 1:6.

The New Testament first and final references:

- First reference: Matthew 5:16 b.
- Final reference: Revelation 14:1.

As a result of all these references, we can get a relatively good understanding of his character and purposes, but the most significant facts about God the Father are found in his relationship with Christ.

## JESUS AND FATHER GOD:

Jesus refers to him as "Father" on all but two of 178 occasions in the Gospels. The two exceptions are found in John 13:1, 3. He mentions him:

- 17 times during the Sermon on the Mount. (Matthew 5–7)
- 22 times in the upper room. (John 13–14)
- 22 times during his final discourse. (John 15–16)
- 6 times during his great high priestly prayer. (John 17)

Jesus began and concluded his ministry by referring to the Father.

- The beginning remark when he was in the temple of Herod:
  *⁴⁹Jesus said to them, "Why were you looking for me? Didn't you know that I must be in my Father's house?"* **Luke 2:49 (NCV)**
- The concluding remark, when he was on the Mount of Olives
  *⁴⁹I will send you what my Father has promised, but you must stay in Jerusalem until you have received that power from heaven."* **Luke 24:49 (NCV)**

## JESUS REVEALS THE CHARACTER OF FATHER GOD:

One of the primary purposes of Christ was to reveal the personhood of his Father. During his ministry, Jesus identified some of these characteristics of his Father.

- He is Spirit. (John 4:24)
- He is invisible. (John 1:18; 6:46)
- He is perfect. (Matt. 5:48)
- He is omnipotent. (Matt. 19:26)
- He is omniscient. (Matt. 10:29-30)
- He is holy. (John 17:11)
- He is righteous. (John 17:25)
- He is loving. (John 3:16; 17:23)
- He is good. (Matt. 6:26, 28-30)

## The Father Supporting His Son:

- He sealed his son: *²⁷Don't work for the food that spoils. Work for the food that stays good always and gives eternal life. The Son of Man will give you this food, because on him God the Father has put his power."* **John 6:27 (NCV)**
- He honored (and honors) his son: *⁵⁴Jesus answered, "If I give honor to myself, that honor is worth nothing. The One who gives me honor is my Father, and you say he is your God.* **John 8:54 (NCV)**
- He bore witness to his son: *¹⁸I am one of the witnesses who speaks about myself, and the Father who sent me is the other witness."* **John 8:18 (NCV)**
- He loved (and loves) his son: *¹⁷The Father loves me because I give my life so that I can take it back again.* **John 10:17 (NCV)**
- He glorified his son: *²⁷"Now I am very troubled. Should I say, 'Father, save me from this time'? No, I came to this time so I could suffer.* **John 12:27 (NCV)**
- He anointed his son: *³⁴The One whom God sent speaks the words of God, because God gives him the Spirit fully. ³⁵The Father loves the Son and has given him power over everything.* **John 3:34-35 (NCV)**
- He taught his son: *²⁸So Jesus said to them, "When you lift up the Son of Man, you will know that I am he. You will know that these things I do are not by my own authority but that I say only what the Father has taught me.* **John 8:28 (NCV)**
- He delighted in his son: *¹⁷And a voice from heaven said, "This is my Son, whom I love, and I am very pleased with him."* **Matthew 3:17(NCV)**
- He was satisfied by his son: *²⁹The One who sent me is with me. I always do what is pleasing to him, so he has not left me alone."* **John 8:29 (NCV)**

## How to be like Father God:

- He sealed his son: Fathers give your children a sense of purpose. Inform them about their destiny as Christians.
- He honored his son: Fathers honor your children by teaching them self-respect. Treat them as a delightful gift from God.
- He bore witness to his son: Fathers support your children by encouraging them in life. Teach them what they need to know to succeed in life as Christians.

- He loves his son: Fathers show your children that you love them. It is not all about discipline. You may spoil the child if you spare the rod, but you will destroy him if you spare your love.

- He glorified his son: Fathers you can support your children by praising their accomplishments and helping them during their challenges. Show them how to become victors instead of victims.

- He anointed his son: Fathers you can anoint your children by empowering them with faith and confidence. Make sure they grow and mature to become part of the church.

- He taught his son: Fathers you must teach your children what it means to be a Christian by your example. Their eyes are on you to demonstrate the character of Christ for them.

- He delighted in his son: Fathers your children look to you for approval! They value your opinion of them, and when you delight yourself in them, you are giving them value in their own eyes.

- He listened to his son: Fathers unless you listen to your children you will never know who they are. It is not just about giving orders.

- He was satisfied by his son: Fathers if your children are doing the best that they can, then be satisfied with their efforts. Don't assume they know you are pleased with them, but rather tell them.

## CONCLUSION:

The father and son relationship of the three persons of the Trinity will always remain a mystery. It is apparent that this relationship had at least one purpose: teaching human fathers how to be fathers to their children. We set our children free to live their own lives. This is a difficult thing to do. In the end, fathers, we can only hope that they have learned from our example and will have loving, happy, and productive lives. We can be assured of this if we have been to them a father like the Father of Jesus! Amen

## NOTES:

# Forty-Eight

## THE VALUE OF THE WORD AND THE SPIRIT

**T**ext: *⁶A voice says, "Cry out!" Then I said, "What shall I cry out?" "Say all people are like the grass, and all their glory is like the flowers of the field. ⁷The grass dies and the flowers fall when the breath of the LORD blows on them. Surely the people are like grass. ⁸The grass dies and the flowers fall, but the word of our God will live forever."* **Isaiah 40:6-8 (NCV)**

*¹So then, rid yourselves of all evil, all lying, hypocrisy, jealousy, and evil speech. ²As newborn babies want milk, you should want the pure and simple teaching. By it you can grow up and be saved, ³because you have already examined and seen how good the Lord is.* **1 Peter 2:1-3 (NCV)**

### INTRODUCTION:
The Word of God must be a foundation for the lifestyle of Christians. The Word contains all the promises and guidance needed for a Christian to live a life pleasing to God. The Word in itself is not enough but must be balanced by interaction with the Holy Spirit. In this sermon, I want to discuss the need for balance, and the characteristics of the Word that make it so valuable to Christians striving to live according to the precepts of God.

### THE BALANCE:
When a church ignores either the Word or the Spirit, it falls out of balance and becomes unhealthy. Once out of balance, two errors can occur in the church:

- If the church ignores the work and manifestation of the Holy Spirit, it can only focus on the law as interpreted by church dogma. Such churches become legalistic and put their members in bondage to the law.
- If the church ignores the Word and concentrates exclusively on the manifestations of the Holy Spirit, it becomes mystical and can easily fall into doctrinal error or heresy.

A healthy church recognizes the interaction between the Word of God and the works of the Holy Spirit. The Word becomes the means of judging the manifestations, and the work of the Holy Spirit becomes the means by which God can directly interact with the people of the church in dramatic and meaningful ways. Keep in mind that the Word becomes the foundation and all else must conform to what it says, but that it is the Holy Spirit who illuminates the Word. Also, remember that the Holy Spirit will never contradict the Word or insist that it is set aside. Because of the predominance of the Word, I would like to explore its characteristics.

## THE SOURCE:
*[21]No prophecy ever came from what a person wanted to say, but people led by the Holy Spirit spoke words from God.* **2 Peter 1:21 (NCV)**

The Word was given to us by God through men who could hear him and interpret his instructions by applying them to the human condition. The fact that the Word came from God has some significant implications.
- The Word is pure and contains no deception or false statements. Therefore, the Word cannot hurt or misguide the reader.
- The Word is living and eternal. As a result, the Word can be applied to all generations regardless of changes in culture or technology. It is living because through the Holy Spirit it is directly connected to the living God who wrote it.

## THE POWER:
The Word contains the power to bring about salvation. It also can change the lifestyle of a person by providing truth to shatter deception. For the Word to have the most significant impact, it must be internalized. Simply reading it or even memorizing it is not enough. The Word must become part of the person. Internalization requires that the person

understand it and appropriate it. It must become the primary resource by which the person makes decisions.

## THE EFFECTS:

The Word has an impact on what we understand about the world and about who we are as humanity. No other source contains such an in-depth description of how God has interacted with people throughout history. The Word reveals our strengths and our weaknesses, our successes and our failures, our resistance to deliverance from our sin nature and our deep hunger for a relationship with God. Because we all have a profound desire to know and be known by God, the Word along with the Holy Spirit can satisfy that desire, and we can be born again and mature into the image of Christ.

## THE ANTAGONISTS:

Peter tells us that certain attitudes and evils can stop the Word from having the desired effect in our lives. These feelings and actions prevent the internalization of the Word:

- Lying: Deception becomes addictive and can block the impact of the Word because the person no longer can speak the truth or know the truth. Lying demands a complex web of deceit, which can blind the person to the truth. The Word is the truth, and someone who has a lifestyle of deception and lying cannot identify the truth.
- Hypocrisy: Saying one thing but doing the opposite. A form of double-mindedness, such a person, cannot appropriate the Word except on a superficial level.
- Jealousy: Jealousy is envy. Envy separates the person from the Word because a person suffering from jealousy also suffers from a lack of love, compassion, and wisdom. The Word becomes useless because the jealous person cannot see beyond his jealousy.
- Evil speech: Evil speech includes slander and bearing false witness. Such behaviors cause the person to become distant from God and his neighbor.

## CONCLUSION:

We must be alert and strive to keep our church and ourselves in a proper balance between the Word and the Holy Spirit lest we fall into error. We need to rid ourselves of any attitude or behavior which prevents us from fully internalizing God's Word. When there is a healthy balance between the Word and the Spirit, we can rejoice in our growth as Christians.

## NOTES:

# *Forty-Nine*

## NOWHERE TO HIDE

**T**ext: *²⁸People did not think it was important to have a true knowledge of God. So God left them and allowed them to have their own worthless thinking and to do things they should not do. ²⁹They are filled with every kind of sin, evil, selfishness, and hatred. They are full of jealousy, murder, fighting, lying, and thinking the worst about each other. They gossip ³⁰and say evil things about each other. They hate God.* **Romans 1:28 (NCV)**

*⁴So, you are not loyal to God! You should know that loving the world is the same as hating God. Anyone who wants to be a friend of the world becomes God's enemy.* **James 4:4 (NCV)**

*¹ LORD, you have examined me and know all about me. ² You know when I sit down and when I get up. You know my thoughts before I think them. ³ You know where I go and where I lie down. You know thoroughly everything I do. ⁴ LORD, even before I say a word, you already know it. ⁵ You are all around me—in front and in back— and have put your hand on me. ⁶ Your knowledge is amazing to me; it is more than I can understand. ⁷ Where can I go to get away from your Spirit? Where can I run from you? If I go up to the heavens, you are there. If I lie down in the grave, you are there. ⁹ If I rise with the sun in the east and settle in the west beyond the sea, ¹⁰ even there you would guide me. With your right hand you would hold me. ¹¹ I could say, "The darkness will hide me. Let the light around me turn into night." ¹² But even the darkness is not dark to you. The night is as light as the day; darkness and light are the same to you.* **Psalms 139:1-12 (NCV)**

*⁹So through Christ we will surely be saved from God's anger, because we have been made right with God by the blood of Christ's death.* **Romans 5:9 (NCV)**

## INTRODUCTION:

Have you attempted to witness to someone who is deeply involved with the world? You may have found it difficult to witness to that person because not only does he think differently, but also acts sinfully with no sense of guilt or shame. Scripture says that such people end up hating God. Scripture also says that God is angry at these people because he has shown them his nature and they still refuse to accept him and walk in a way that pleases him. In this sermon, I want to look at ways that people react to their lack of a relationship with God, and how we can understand their spiritual condition,

## INITIAL CAUSES:

According to Romans: *²⁸People did not think it was important to have a true knowledge of God. So God left them and allowed them to have their own worthless thinking and to do things they should not do.* **Romans 1:28 (NCV)**

The conflict between God and humanity began when people rejected the knowledge of God.

- They dismissed his holiness and his divine will, and their need for him.
- They became self-willed and began to behave in ways that pleased themselves but rejected God.
- They attempted to substitute a relationship with God with sinful desires and behaviors.
- God allowed them to suffer the consequences of their rejection of all that he valued and desired to see regarding humanities growth and social progress.
- Their sin made God angry enough to reject them.
- God still loved them even in their sin, but he rejected fellowship with them.
- Because they suffer the consequences of their sin, they blame God and begin to hate him and those that represent them. This hate explains the worldwide persecution of Christians.

Jerome A. Jochem M.S., M.A.

## LOVING THE WORLD:

We are commanded by Christ first to love God and then love each other. When people ignore these two commandments, then they suffer the consequences. People try to fill the need to love God by getting involved with the worldly behaviors that are sinful. Such sins can be cataloged as follows:

- Evil is any action which breaks God's law or is a rebellion against his standards of conduct.
- Selfishness is evaluating oneself as being better than others, so you disregard their needs.
- Hatred is the emotional justification for violent behavior.
- Jealousy is envy about what someone else has or how he is treated by others.
- Murder and fighting is aggression either verbal or physical that can result in someone dying or getting hurt.
- Lying is distorting the truth for self-gain.
- Thinking the worst thoughts about each other. The act of negatively judging others.
- Gossip is communicating false information or lies about others.
- The hate of God is the angry rejection of God and aggression against believers.

## NOWHERE TO HIDE:

One of the most common responses resulting from living a life of sin is to try to hide from God. Hiding from God is an attempt to avoid the negative consequences of sin. One of the initial responses of Adam and Eve after they disobeyed God, was to hide from God. (Genesis 3:8). Hiding from God includes such attitudes and behaviors as denying that he exists, believing that he does not care because he is remote and distant, and assuming that he will not be able to bring about the consequences of sin. It is impossible to hide from God for three reasons, all of which have to do with his attributes.

- First of all, he is omnipresent. That means that he exists everywhere and therefore there is nowhere to hide.
- Second of all, he is omniscient. That means that he knows everything, including the nature of the sin and when an individual sins against him.

- Thirdly, he is omnipotent. That means that he has all power to bring about consequences related to sin.

## GOD'S SOLUTION:

Our anger and rejection of God and God's anger at us are resolved only through the sacrifice of our Lord Jesus Christ when he became a substitute for us and for the punishment we deserve. We cannot hide our sin from God, but we can claim the blood of Jesus so that he will forgive us our sins against him instead of remaining angry at us for our trespasses.

## CONCLUSION:

We cannot sacrifice our relationship with God for anything that the world offers us. To do so is to reject God and all the blessings and promises that he gives us. When we do sin, we need to depend upon God's forgiveness through Jesus Christ. That means that we must first of all confess and then repent of our sin. We must remember that there is nowhere we can run to, or anyplace that we can hide from God. So, we must have the courage to admit our sin and depend on God to forgive us.

## NOTES:

# TRUSTING

**T**ext: *⁷"But the person who trusts in the LORD will be blessed. The LORD will show him that he can be trusted.* **Jeremiah 17:7 (NCV)**

*¹³We know that we live in God and he lives in us, because he gave us his Spirit. ¹⁴We have seen and can testify that the Father sent his Son to be the Savior of the world. ¹⁵Whoever confesses that Jesus is the Son of God has God living inside, and that person lives in God. ¹⁶And so we know the love that God has for us, and we trust that love.* **1 John 4:13-16 (NCV)**

*⁵ Trust the LORD with all your heart, and don't depend on your own understanding. ⁶ Remember the LORD in all you do, and he will give you success. ⁷Don't depend on your own wisdom. Respect the LORD and refuse to do wrong. ⁸ Then your body will be healthy, and your bones will be strong.* **Proverbs 3:5-8 (NCV)**

## INTRODUCTION:

In Scripture, the word "trust" is used interchangeably with the word "faith." That is because when we talk about the trust that such people as Abraham had in God, we are also talking about his faith in God's promises. There is a difference between the two words. Faith tends to refer to what a person believes, while trust is concerned with what a person does. So, faith in God demands that you trust him, and you express that trust through both submission and obedience. Trust between God and people can't exist unless they have trust in him, and he can trust us. In this sermon, I would like to explore this dual relationship and outline the benefits of trusting God.

## BLESSING FROM TRUSTING THE LORD:

Trust does not come quickly to most of us. It is fundamental to human nature that we do not trust each other. In many instances, our lack of trust grows from the fact that it is violated so often by others. What Scripture tells us is that other people may break faith with us, but we can trust God and in doing so obtain many blessings such as:

- Protection. We can be protected from the traps and machinations of our enemy the Devil.
- Faithfulness. We learn faithfulness by experiencing the faithfulness of God.
- Wisdom. God can be trusted to give us the understanding to make the correct choices in life.
- God's Love. God loves us, and we can depend on that love to continue eternally.
- Happiness. Placing trust in God means that we have a particular joy in living.
- Salvation. We receive salvation not by works, but by trusting in his grace.
- Provision. We can trust God to meet both our physical and spiritual needs.
- Hope. In a world that has no hope, trusting God gives us hope for eternity.
- Success. This means spiritual as well as material success in life.

Why does God give us all these blessings? He is demonstrating to us that we can trust him in every area of our lives. As we begin to trust him is small things, then our faith becomes stronger. God is not trying to bribe us to trust him. Instead, he is giving us a foundation of trust to stand on in our voyage through life.

## THE KEY IS LOVE:

The people that we must trust the most are the people we want to love the most. These people are also the most difficult to believe because love demands transparency and self-revelation. In most relationships, trust slowly develops as we become confident that the person loves us. God knows this, and so he provided a way for us to experience his love and then trust him with our love. He builds our trust by:

- Giving us the Holy Spirit who expresses his love for us as an emotion.
- Reassuring us that we have a real unity with him by frequently sharing his presence.

As his relationship with us develops, we will become more confident and convicted that he loves us and we trust him with every aspect of our lives.

## WISDOM BASED ON TRUST:

We all want to live productive and joyful lives, and that takes wisdom. Wisdom to make correct decisions in life. Knowledge about getting along with people and how to raise a family. Just dealing with children demands a wealth of understanding. Verse 5 of our final text for today tells us that we should: *5 Trust the LORD with all your heart, and don't depend on your own understanding.* Getting to the point of trusting with all our hearts is sometimes a challenge because:

- We may not trust anyone but ourselves. To trust in God becomes a difficult step to take in our spiritual growth.
- Even if we have learned to trust God in some things, we may not trust him in everything.
- We may depend on our limited knowledge and information instead of trusting God who knows everything and can do anything.
- We are taught to be independent and self-reliant, and we don't even attempt to seek guidance from God.
- We may seek wisdom from others who do not have the understanding or knowledge to help us.

To be wise, we must depend on the intelligence and knowledge that only God possesses. Seeking his wisdom brings the rewards of a healthy and joyful life.

## CONCLUSION:

Seeking the wisdom of God does not come easily or naturally. The only way we can obtain that wisdom is by involving God in our daily lives and by seeking his counsel in every decision that we make. Scripture tells us that God will never fail or deceive us so we can make his holiness and faithfulness the foundation of our trust.

NOTES:

# *Fifty-One*

## MARRIAGE OR MARRIAGE RENEWAL SERVICE

**W**elcome:
      On behalf of _____ and _____, I welcome you to this their marriage (renewal) ceremony. It is a celebration of a marriage (that has lasted for _____ years,) and it is also the celebration of the miracle of love. We must remember that what we do here today, is not done only in the sight of witnesses, but also in the sight of the Lord Jesus Christ.

**SONG SELECTION:** (TBA by Couple)

**SCRIPTURE READING:**
_____ and _____, today, in the presence of the Holy Spirit, we celebrate this miracle in your lives. Scripture says: *⁴Love is patient and kind. Love is not jealous, it does not brag, and it is not proud.*

*⁵Love is not rude, is not selfish, and does not get upset with others. Love does not count up wrongs that have been done. ⁶Love is not happy with evil but is happy with the truth. ⁷Love patiently accepts all things. It always trusts, always hopes, and always remains strong. ⁸Love never ends.*
**1 Corinthians 13:4-8 (NCV)**

**INSTRUCTION:**
Learning to love each other, to talk to each other, and to live together in harmony are some of the most important challenges of marriage. As you will learn, we can't treat marriage frivolously. Marriage requires

daily care, and we are to embrace marriage with enduring integrity at all times.

_____and _____, I charge you both as you stand in the presence of God, to remember that love, trust, and faithfulness to each other and God are the basis of a jubilant and lasting marriage. These vows you are about to make are hallowed. If these pledges are uninterrupted, and as you work to do the will of our Lord Jesus Christ, you will experience a marriage filled with joy and love.

VOWS: (Vows written by the couple or standard vows may be used.)

## RING SERVICE:
These rings are symbols of eternity and the unbroken circle of love. Love, which is not based on conditions, but is given freely in every situation you experience during your life together. When you look at your ring, remember your vows shall not be broken.

**(Insert the first name of the man and then repeat using the first name of bride)**

_____ as you place this treasured ring on _____ finger, repeat after me: Just as this ring encircles your finger, so does my love embraces your heart. This ring is a symbol of my love for you, and this ring confirms my increasing love for you. With this ring, I seal my vows to you and I thee wed.

## THE CEREMONY OF FAMILY UNION:
Candle Service:
At this point, three or more candles (one for each family and a central candle representing the new family) may be lit after a brief introduction of the meaning given by the pastor.
Sand Service:
A sand service may also be used here. Three or more different colored sands are poured into a central glass container. The first partial pour is made by the couple, followed by each family or child pouring in their colored sand. Finally, the couple pours the remainder of their sand into the container. The pastor should explain the meaning of this service

Jerome A. Jochem M.S., M.A.

## FINAL STATEMENT:

As you walk through your voyage together, please remember these fundamental values that result in a lasting marriage and continued love:

To love is to listen - it is the little things said in love that keep you bonded together.

To love is to forgive - neither of you is perfect, so offense must be forgiven.

To love is to be self-revealing - being transparent because you intimately trust each other.

To love is to share - giving to each other freely and without restriction.

## BLESSING:

May your love never fade, may you never take each other for granted and when you are old, may you be found, hand in hand, still thanking God for each other. Always treat each other with tenderness, kindness, respect, and remind yourselves often of your love.

## DECLARATION:

_____ and _____, you have consented together in holy matrimony before God, have pledged your vows to each other, and have exchanged rings as tokens of your love and commitment to each other. In accordance with the laws of _____ (State), with the authority invested in me by the _____, (Church Denomination or Fellowship) and with great joy, I now confirm that you are husband and wife. The Lord bless you and keep you; The Lord make His face shine upon you and be gracious to you; The Lord lift up His countenance upon you and give you peace.

**COMMUNION:** (It is essential that the couple is trained in taking communion during rehearsal)

**ANNOUNCEMENT:** Congratulations. Ladies and Gentlemen, I introduce to you Mr. and Mrs. _____

**NOTE:** You may print this page in landscape format so that it fits in your Bible.

# Fifty-Two

## FUNERAL SERMON

**P**reparation Note: Before you begin this sermon, read the obituary and gather facts about the family and accomplishments of the deceased person. Keep in mind that you are dealing with grief and so this may not be the time to present a strong or long evangelism message without bringing comfort and hope to those in attendance, especially family members. Keep it simple, focus on heaven and not on hell, and do not preach for an eternity. This funeral service is for those who have made a commitment to Jesus and are saved. It may be modified, however, if the salvation of the deceased is uncertain and you are addressing Christians and non-Christians attending the funeral. If you do not know whether the dead person was saved, don't condemn him, but leave all judgment to God.

**The Order of the Service:** Determine the order of the service by talking to family members, especially, the person in charge of the funeral. The funeral director will be of great help in this matter. Often the family will want unique music played or will want to talk about the deceased person or have a special prayer said. This sermon outline may be modified to fit the order of service.

**Prayer:** Pray that those who are attending will hear this message. Also, pray for the broken hearts of the family and friends of the deceased person. Make this a spontaneous prayer as the Holy Spirit leads you. You may give the obituary either before or after the prayer.

Jerome A. Jochem M.S., M.A.

**Text:** *²⁰When Martha heard that Jesus was coming, she went out to meet him, but Mary stayed home. ²¹Martha said to Jesus, "Lord, if you had been here, my brother would not have died.*

*²²But I know that even now God will give you anything you ask." ²³Jesus said, "Your brother will rise and live again." ²⁴Martha answered, "I know that he will rise and live again in the resurrection[£] on the last day." ²⁵Jesus said to her, "I am the resurrection and the life. Those who believe in me will have life even if they die. ²⁶And everyone who lives and believes in me will never die. Martha, do you believe this?" ²⁷Martha answered, "Yes, Lord. I believe that you are the Christ, the Son of God, the One coming to the world."* **John 11:20-27 (NCV)**

## The Promise: For the Living and the Dead.
*I am the resurrection and the life. Those who believe in me will have life even if they die. (Vs. 25)*
- Every one of us shall die, yet Jesus promised us life.
- Death is not the end, but a new beginning.
- With whom do we live – Jesus
- Where do we live – In heaven, where Jesus lives.
- We say farewell to the remains of _____, but know that one day we will see her/him again.

## The Condition of the Promise
*²And everyone who lives and believes in me will never die. (Vs. 26a)*

This part of the Scripture directly applies to us because we live.
- It is the same promise with the same condition.
- It is for those who believe in Jesus as their Savior and Lord.
- Savior means you accept that Jesus died to deliver you from sin.
- Lord means that he is your "boss" directing your life and walk.

## The Question:
*Martha, do you believe this? (Vs. 26b)*

Another way of asking this question is this: are you trusting in Jesus to give you eternal life.

- Trusting him means that you have made a commitment to him or that you are placing your faith in him.
- No one else or nothing else will give you eternal life. That includes wealth, power, or religion.
- Listen to what Jesus said: *⁶Jesus answered, "I am the way, and the truth, and the life. The only way to the Father is through me.* **John 14:6 (NCV)**

## THE ACTION:
- If you want eternal life in heaven with Jesus, then you must first turn your life and then your will over to him.
- You must accept the cross as a way to get to heaven and then develop a relationship with Jesus that will last until your day draws near.
- So here is the question: have you made that commitment, and are you walking with Jesus?

**Invitation:** Invite people to accept Jesus and gain eternal life. Make sure you follow up after the service so that you can instruct those who made a confession of faith as to the next steps to be taken.

## FINAL PRAYER:
Dear Lord Jesus, today we commit the physical remains of _____ to the earth, for it is written that from dust we came and to dust we return. But we do this with the confident hope, and firm faith that _____ is rejoicing with you in heaven. We believe in your promise of eternal life because we believe in you. Now I thank you for your divine presence here with us and ask that as we leave this gravesite, you will go with us. I pray that you will be with us until that day that you take us by the hand, and lead us to our heavenly home which you have prepared for us. In the Name of Jesus, we pray.
Amen.

## NOTES:

Printed in the United States
By Bookmasters